Missiles in Cuba

MISSILES IN CUBA

*Kennedy, Khrushchev, Castro
and the 1962 Crisis*

Mark J. White

The American Ways Series

IVAN R. DEE   *Chicago*

Library of Congress Cataloging-in-Publication Data:
White, Mark J.
    Missiles in Cuba : Kennedy, Khrushchev, Castro and the 1962
crisis / Mark J. White.
        p.   cm. — (The American ways series)
    Includes bibliographical references and index.
    ISBN 1-56663-155-6 (cloth : alk. paper). — ISBN 1-56663-156-4
(paper : alk. paper)
    1. Cuban Missile Crisis, 1962.   I. Title.   II. Series.
E841.W49   1997
973.922—dc21   96-54620

For R. A. White and N. J. White

Contents

Preface

HISTORIANS HAVE recently redefined their work on the Cuban missile crisis in a chronological sense. For many years they concentrated on those thirteen days in October 1962 when the world came to the brink of nuclear war. This focus has now been supplemented by an equally intense interest in the roots of the crisis. Thus this book devotes two chapters to the roles played by the United States and the Soviet Union (and to a lesser extent, Cuba) in bringing on the crisis, and a third chapter to those crucial few weeks immediately preceding it.

I have made use of the great number of books and articles written by historians and political scientists on the missile crisis, and memoirs by participants. But many important documents have recently been made available and have not yet been incorporated into historical and analytical accounts. For this book I have examined the new documentation, which includes materials on Operation Mongoose from the National Security Archive in Washington, D.C.; tapes of the October 18 and 22, 1962, ExComm meetings from the John F. Kennedy Library, Boston; and correspondence between Soviet officials in Washington and Havana and their colleagues in Moscow that has been published under the auspices of the Cold War International History Project of the Woodrow Wilson Center.

My thanks to John Braeman and Ivan Dee for their generosity and expertise. I am indebted to the School of History and International Relations at the University of St. Andrews for a grant that enabled me to conduct research in Washington, D.C. William Burr and Ian Stevenson of the National Security Archive, and James Hershberg, have directed my attention to many important materials; their assistance has been invaluable. And I am grateful to Steve Spackman for his support and wise counsel at an important time.

                                                              M. J. W.

Charleston, Illinois
January 1997

Missiles in Cuba

1

Background to Crisis

AT THE START OF 1959 an uprising in Cuba, led by the dynamic young revolutionary leader Fidel Castro, resulted in the overthrow of Fulgencio Batista, the country's long-time corrupt dictator. From that moment the United States was faced with a dilemma in the Caribbean that in many ways represented the central challenge for American foreign policymakers in the twentieth century—how to respond to revolution.

The United States was itself the product of a successful revolution, one of watershed importance in that it signaled the shift away from the *ancien régime* to a new liberal, middle-class order in the Western world. Less than a decade after defeating Britain in the War of Independence, however, Americans observed events in France after 1789 and wondered whether revolution was a good thing. Some political leaders, notably Thomas Jefferson, generally applauded the French revolutionaries as akin to America's Founding Fathers. Others, such as Alexander Hamilton, were appalled by France's violence and social upheaval.

By the twentieth century this American ambivalence toward revolution had become an almost total repulsion. Whereas earlier revolutions, such as those in Europe in 1848, might be interpreted as promoting the sort of liberal-capitalist order congenial to the United States, those after 1900, such as the Bolshevik Revolution in Russia in 1917, often seemed to bring about state-dominated, anticapitalist economic policies and dictatorships rather than democratically elected leaderships. The onset of the cold war after World War II, and the accompanying fear among Americans that their chief adversary, the Soviet Union, was actively promoting the Communist movement overseas, made American leaders even more wary of revolution. Thus in the twentieth century the United States emerged as the world's leading status quo power, and particularly so after 1945.

Nowhere was American determination to maintain order and stability stronger than in the Caribbean. The geographic proximity of that area meant that the application of military, political, or economic pressure from Washington was usually a simple matter. This was especially true for the island of Cuba, located only ninety miles off the Florida coast. In 1898 President William McKinley had intervened in the conflict raging between Cuba and its colonial master, Spain. After defeating the Spanish and acquiring a number of territorial possessions in the process, the United States technically granted Cuba its independence. In reality, however, Cuba became an American protectorate. The decades after 1898 saw the United States deploy troops on the island on several occasions, a policy sanctioned in 1901 by the U.S. Senate.

When Castro came to power, the administration of Republican President Dwight D. Eisenhower, at the midpoint of his second term, was unsure how to respond. On the one hand, Castro held out a promise of genuine democracy. He talked of free elections and initially appointed a number of Cuban liberals to important positions in his government. On the other hand, he appeared at the very least to accept that Communists would play a significant role in the new Cuba, especially when in mid-January 1961 he legalized the Communist party.

In recent years it has been fashionable for historians to applaud Eisenhower's foreign policy. He has been portrayed as a cautious, skillful statesman, one who managed both to stand up to the Communists when necessary and to defuse dangerous cold war crises, such as the 1958–1959 dispute over access to Berlin. But Eisenhower's record on Cuba does not lend support to such a positive interpretation. Although Castro often provided him with good reason, Eisenhower's policy toward Cuba's new leader was one of swiftly escalating hostility. In many ways the tactics he adopted in dealing with Castro set the tone for the policies of his successor.

In March 1960 Eisenhower approved a Central Intelligence Agency (CIA) "program" for Cuba which included the creation of "a paramilitary force outside of Cuba for future guerrilla action." Implementing that directive, by late summer the CIA had established a training camp in Guatemala for a group of Cuban exiles. This initiative laid the groundwork for what would later become an abortive invasion of Cuba, the Bay of Pigs operation. But this was only one ingredient in Eisenhower's anti-Castro policy mix. In the summer of 1960 he introduced what he himself described as "economic sanctions." He cut the amount of sugar imported from Cuba as retaliation for Castro's decision to take control of the oil refineries of Shell and other American companies in Cuba. Eisenhower broke off diplomatic relations with Cuba in January 1961 after Castro ordered most of the personnel in the American embassy in Havana off the island. In addition to all this, the CIA began devising plots to assassinate Castro, though the extent of Eisenhower's knowledge of them is not clear, while contingency plans for the direct use of American force against Cuba were developed in the Defense

Department. Hence Eisenhower bequeathed to his successor a Cuban policy based on the application of covert, economic, diplomatic, and potential military pressure.

Eisenhower's successor was John F. Kennedy, the youthful and charismatic senator from Massachusetts who had enjoyed a meteoric rise to prominence. Kennedy, just forty-three, had grown up in a Boston Irish family with an established political pedigree in Massachusetts and an ever-increasing fortune built by the patriarch, Joseph Kennedy. JFK was educated at exclusive private schools before going on to Harvard. Service during World War II, for which he was decorated, preceded his election in 1946 as a Democrat to the House of Representatives. After six lazy, undistinguished years in the House, Kennedy was elected in 1952 to the Senate after scoring a surprise victory over his formidable Republican opponent, Henry Cabot Lodge.

By the mid-1950s Kennedy had emerged as one of the Democratic party's leading figures. The publication of a Pulitzer Prize–winning book, *Profiles in Courage*, added immensely to his credibility, even though some doubted the extent of Kennedy's authorship, a skepticism that historians have echoed. At the 1956 Democratic convention in Chicago, Kennedy failed narrowly to become the vice-presidential nominee after Adlai Stevenson decided to allow convention delegates to choose his running mate. Kennedy sustained his high profile during the late 1950s by embarking on political trips and making speeches across the nation.

Some recent presidents, such as Jimmy Carter and Bill Clinton, have entered the White House without having devoted much time to an examination of foreign policy. JFK certainly did not fall into that category. From an early age he had grappled with the prominent international issues of the day and had reached some conclusions about how a great power like the United States should act on the world's stage. These conclusions shaped his policies as president.

As with so many other Americans who lived through that decade, the 1930s had an indelible impact on Kennedy's thinking. The key international development of those years was the failure of appeasement to satisfy Adolf Hitler's expansionist ambitions, and the consequence of World War II. Not interested simply as a lay observer in those events, Kennedy embarked on a detailed study of the British appeasement of Germany in the thesis he submitted for his undergraduate degree at Harvard. He had spent time in England during his father's stint as President Franklin D. Roosevelt's ambassador there from 1937 to 1940. With the help of his father, JFK found a publisher for his thesis. The book, published in 1940, was called *Why England Slept*. It reveals much about the direction of Kennedy's early thinking on foreign and defense policy.

One of the most important aspects of *Why England Slept* was its comparison of democracies such as Britain and totalitarian powers such as Nazi Germany. The British government, Kennedy noted, was subject to pressures from various interest groups and public opinion against an arms buildup; Hitler did not have to tolerate such pressures. For this reason the German government was able to increase military spending without impediment while London could not. Thus at the end of the 1930s British defenses were ill-prepared to meet the challenge posed by a Germany that was by then heavily armed. Kennedy concluded that when dealing with totalitarian foes, liberal democracies needed the strength of purpose and clarity of vision to increase military spending and adopt a generally tough, uncompromising outlook, whatever the magnitude of domestic opposition.

That conclusion seemed to Kennedy to have special rele-

vance to the U.S. position after World War II. At the time of
his election to the House of Representatives, the Soviet-American partnership that had been centrally important to the defeat of Germany, Italy, and Japan had begun to deteriorate
into a state of mutual hostility that would soon become known
as the cold war. Just as Britain had faced Nazi Germany during the 1930s, so the United States was now compelled to confront an equally implacable totalitarian foe in the form of the
Soviet Union. Recalling the lessons he had learned from his
analysis of appeasement, Congressman Kennedy called for a
vigorous response to the Soviet challenge and emphasized the
importance of greater American military spending. While
many political figures were demanding the same things during the tense early years of the cold war, JFK's speeches in the
House of Representatives during the late 1940s and early
1950s were exceptionally harsh. He often criticized Democratic President Harry S. Truman for failing to meet the Soviet challenge with sufficient forcefulness.

During the 1950s Kennedy diluted his hard-line foreign
policy views. His trips overseas, notably one to the Middle and
Far East in 1951, proved educative. JFK now understood that
in many cases the success of the left in the Third World was
due more to strong, indigenous anticolonial movements than
to meddling from Moscow. Anxious to court liberal Democrats as he began to think in terms of a White House bid,
Kennedy also started to offer at least lip service and perhaps
serious consideration to the idea of a treaty limiting nuclear
testing and to the general notion of nuclear disarmament.

In the 1950s the Democratic party developed deep divisions
on international issues. One wing of the party, led by former
Secretary of State Dean Acheson, argued that vast military
power and an unremitting hostility toward the Soviet bloc
should characterize American foreign policy. The other wing,

dominated by Adlai Stevenson, stressed the importance of using economic aid and diplomacy, not just the threat of force, in combating communism around the world.

Although Kennedy showed sympathy for the alternative path laid down by Stevenson and others, he was generally more comfortable with the traditional cold war views articulated by the Acheson wing. What helped to cement his attitude was the emergence of the "missile gap" theory in the late 1950s. When the Soviet Union developed its own intercontinental ballistic missile (ICBM) and successfully launched Sputnik, the world's first man-made satellite, both in 1957, many in the United States became convinced that Moscow was winning the arms race. We now know (as did President Eisenhower at the time, from intelligence data not released to the American public) that the Soviets still lagged far behind the United States in nuclear weaponry. Yet many critics of Eisenhower, including Kennedy, admonished him for refusing to bolster military spending in order to close the "gap." In this way JFK returned at the end of the 1950s to the theme he had developed in 1940 in *Why England Slept*, namely the importance of military preparedness. Although many observers after the tragedy of his assassination in 1963 would portray Kennedy as a president intent on ending or at least curbing the excesses of the cold war, the man who announced his candidacy for president in January 1960 was in fact a rather traditional cold warrior.

That 1960 campaign, because of the public commitments he made on Cuba, almost certainly played a role in shaping Kennedy's handling of Castro after the election. Richard Nixon, Kennedy's Republican rival and Eisenhower's vice-president, had made a career of railing against communism and those Democrats he regarded as "soft" on it. Kennedy was determined to stop Nixon from using the same tactics against him. In his campaign, therefore, JFK criticized Nixon for his involvement in an administration that had allowed the "missile gap" to develop and permitted Castro to win power in Cuba. Kennedy promised swift action to remove Castro. On October 20, for instance, the night before his final television debate with Nixon, he declared that "we must attempt to strengthen the non-Batista democratic anti-Castro forces in exile, and in Cuba itself, who offer eventual hope of overthrowing Castro. Thus far these fighters for freedom have had virtually no support from our Government." Many Americans voted on election day knowing that Kennedy was dissatisfied with the Eisenhower-Nixon policy toward Cuba and that he had promised to expand the effort to oust Castro. This election promise may well have encouraged JFK during his presidency to implement the sort of hostile, anti-Castro policies he soon came to favor.

After narrowly defeating Nixon, the president-elect assembled his administration. In foreign policy the key appointments were Dean Rusk as secretary of state, Robert McNamara as secretary of defense, McGeorge Bundy as special assistant for national security affairs, and, though it was not then clear from the position he was given, his younger brother, Robert Kennedy, as attorney general. President Kennedy also decided to retain the services of Allen Dulles and Richard Bissell at the CIA.

After the creation of the National Security Council in 1947, the State Department had often had to fight to retain its traditional authority in matters of foreign policy. Under Rusk's leadership, the State Department lost that battle during the Kennedy years. Bundy proved to be a more dynamic and influential figure than Rusk; besides, JFK wanted to be his own secretary of state. In addition, McNamara came to play a crucial role not only on defense matters but in foreign policy as well. Indeed, with the possible exception of Robert Kennedy, who was clearly the closest adviser to his brother and whose policy domain after April 1961 included international issues such as Cuba, McNamara emerged as the most influential voice within the new administration.

An important characteristic of Kennedy's administration, one that both reflected the foreign policy ideology of the new president and affected his policies, was the absence of liberal Democrats in key positions. Adlai Stevenson, regarded by many as the party's best-informed thinker on international affairs, was named ambassador to the United Nations, a position that allowed him to maintain a high public profile but provided him with little real influence in the policymaking process. Chester Bowles, as under secretary of state, was the only liberal to be given a position of potentially considerable influence; but he lasted less than a year in that office. Men such as Stevenson and Bowles believed in negotiations with Moscow and Havana and in economic rather than military means to fight the cold war. Their peripheral position within the new administration suggested that those approaches would not become central motifs of Kennedy's foreign policy.

Kennedy's main objectives, certainly up to the time of the Cuban missile crisis, were to promote a large military buildup and to advance unyielding policies toward cold war adversaries. Despite learning on becoming president that the United States was far ahead in the arms race—or, to put it another way, that the "missile gap" was false—JFK nonetheless pressed ahead with major increases in defense spending, for conventional forces as well as nuclear armaments. Unlike Eisenhower, he also decided to make public the fact that the Soviet Union was losing the arms race to the United States. Although he consistently refused to deploy combat troops in South Vietnam to help defeat the Communists there, he deep-

ened American involvement in that country by sending increasing numbers of U.S. military advisers and special forces.
In 1961 Kennedy responded to Khrushchev's threat to eliminate the Western presence in Berlin by preparing the United
States for a military confrontation in Europe.

JFK's handling of Castro was consistent with his overall
foreign policy. Up to the time of the missile crisis, Kennedy
employed every conceivable method to overthrow Castro,
apart from a direct American attack on Cuba (though even
that was maintained as an option).

JFK's determination to overthrow Castro derived from a
number of concerns. He believed the Cuban leader had allowed his country to become a Soviet satellite, and that Castro's regime might produce a spate of revolutions throughout
Latin America. Viewing Cuba through the prism of his 1930s
experiences, JFK had the general sense that a dictator such as
Castro should not be tolerated. Kennedy also knew only too
well that his failure to oust the Cuban leader, especially given
the stand he had taken against Castro during the 1960 presidential campaign, would encourage Republican critics.

Having decided that Castro must go, Kennedy sought to
accomplish his objective by both overt and covert means, but
mainly the latter. He was attracted to secret operations for
various reasons. For one thing, they could be pursued without
the need to explain the underlying policy to the American
people or the international community. For another, Kennedy
came to the presidency with considerable faith in the compe-
tence of CIA officials, the government's covert specialists who
had managed in the 1950s to topple undesirable governments
in Iran and Guatemala. In addition, JFK felt that the Soviet
Union often sought to expand its influence in underhanded
ways; hence it was important for the United States to respond
in kind. A speech by Nikita S. Khrushchev on January 6,

1961, in which the Soviet premier asserted his determination to support not local or world wars but wars of national liberation, which he defined as "uprisings of colonial peoples against their oppressors, developing into guerrilla wars," confirmed for Kennedy the need to employ covert tactics against a covert threat.

Kennedy's first attempt to overthrow Castro surreptitiously was the CIA-organized Bay of Pigs invasion in April 1961, an attempt to foment an uprising against the Cuban leader by returning a group of anti-Castro Cuban exiles to their homeland. Although that operation failed and became a huge public embarrassment for the president, it should be recalled that Kennedy's hope, even his assumption, was that the plan would be carried out *without* the American public or the international community learning that his administration had orchestrated the invasion.

As many Kennedy supporters are quick to point out, the plan that later became the Bay of Pigs operation was first developed during the final months of Eisenhower's second term. By the time JFK became president, the operation had acquired a momentum of its own. Some of his advisers felt it needed to be authorized quickly, within a few weeks of the new administration coming to office. Kennedy would have needed great independence of mind to reject a plan endorsed by CIA legends Dulles and Bissell and apparently supported by Eisenhower, a military hero.

Evidence reveals, however, that JFK had more time to consider the idea of using Cuban exiles in an invasion of their homeland than the twelve weeks between his inauguration and the invasion at the Bay of Pigs. By 1960 it was the custom for incumbent chief executives to grant national security briefings to presidential candidates. On Eisenhower's instructions, therefore, Allen Dulles spoke to Kennedy in late July and mid-September 1960. Dulles's notes in preparation for the July meeting reveal he intended to inform JFK that the CIA was training Cuban exiles, and Robert Kennedy later confirmed that his brother knew about the scheme before the November election. Thus when JFK authorized the landing at the Bay of Pigs in April 1961 he had been able to ponder the plan in general outline for fully nine months.

A more common defense of Kennedy's decision to carry out the Bay of Pigs plan is that no one, with the exception of William Fulbright, chairman of the Senate Foreign Relations Committee, advised him to cancel it. But Dean Acheson explained his misgivings about the plan to Kennedy, as did White House aide Arthur Schlesinger. Chester Bowles also opposed the plan, and his dissent was passed on to the president. In meetings of senior officials during the early days of the administration, Rusk and his State Department colleagues argued that the invasion would damage the U.S. position throughout Latin America and in the United Nations. Many other officials also found fault with the plan, and several who probably would have, such as Stevenson and Special Counsel Theodore Sorensen, received only partial briefings or none at all. In short, a good many officials opposed the Bay of Pigs operation. JFK approved the invasion knowing that support for it within his administration was less than solid.

Kennedy significantly reduced any chance of success for the plan by the way he modified it. Originally the idea was for the exiles to land on Cuba's south coast, at Trinidad. But the president wanted the operation carried out with the minimum of fanfare so that American backing for it remained hidden. At his insistence the CIA moved the beachhead for the invasion thirty-five miles west to the Bay of Pigs, an area less densely populated than Trinidad. The premise of the operation, however, was that a small invasion would be effective because it could provoke an anti-Castro uprising. In an area as thinly populated as the Bay of Pigs, that was never likely to happen.

After Kennedy gave his final approval, the operation began on April 15, 1961, when six B-26 bombers, with fake markings to suggest that the pilots had defected from Castro's air force, took off from Nicaragua on a mission to strike Cuba's major airfields. They were only partially successful, and some of Castro's jets that survived were later used to good effect by the Cuban leader. The Cuban exile brigade, which had been trained in Guatemala, tried to land at the Bay of Pigs on the night of April 16–17. But Castro, who had already mobilized his militia, was able to dispatch forces quickly to the beach-head. At the same time he ordered the detainment of 100,000 Cubans who were allegedly opposed to his rule and who might have supported an anti-Castro uprising. A decision by JFK to cancel air attacks on Castro's main airfields—on April 17 for political reasons and on April 18 because of bad weather—did not help the plight of the invaders. By April 19 it was clear that the Bay of Pigs invasion had failed. About 100 of the invaders had been killed and roughly 1,200 taken prisoner.

What doubled Kennedy's discomfort was that American backing for the operation soon became public knowledge. Cuba wasted no time in bringing the matter to the attention of the United Nations. JFK tried to minimize the political damage by publicly taking full responsibility for the disaster; nevertheless it was a personal setback. Many Americans felt at the time of his election that he lacked the experience and maturity to be president. The Bay of Pigs seemed to validate that suspicion.

As the operation fizzled out, Kennedy now needed to decide how to handle Castro in the wake of the Bay of Pigs failure. Those he consulted recommended radically different approaches. Inside his administration, Robert Kennedy called for an invasion of Cuba, arguing that "we would have to act or be judged paper tigers by Moscow." Some leading Republicans offered the president similar advice. Nixon, for example, supported military action against Cuba.

Kennedy's liberal advisers urged him to show greater restraint. Richard Goodwin, his assistant special counsel, felt that the acceleration of the Alliance for Progress, the economic aid program for Latin America that JFK had announced in March, was the best means to ensure that Castro's influence did not spread throughout the Western Hemisphere. Stevenson also suggested to Kennedy that economic aid for developing nations, rather than "gunboat diplomacy" against Cuba, should be the order of the day. The application of diplomatic pressure on Cuba through the Organization of American States (OAS) was Chester Bowles's preferred course of action.

In the end JFK agreed with the objective his hard-line advisers had defined, namely the quick overthrow of Castro. But he decided to rely mainly on clandestine means rather than the open use of American force to achieve that goal. A direct assault on Cuba was still to be retained as a policy option (a May 5 National Security Action Memorandum made clear that nothing would be done to "foreclose the possibility of military intervention in the future"), but for the next year and a half Kennedy and his chief advisers would rely on covert pressure to loosen Castro's grip. In addition, planning for the possible use of force against Cuba was authorized. And during this period the CIA devised plots to assassinate Castro, though the degree of JFK's knowledge of these plans is not clear.

The development of contingency plans for military action against Cuba had begun as early as November 1959 under the supervision of Admiral Robert Lee Dennison, commander-in-chief of Atlantic forces. From that point until the missile crisis itself, three basic plans were formulated and honed. The first, known as Operation Plan 312 (or OPLAN 312), was a "fast reaction air strike." The second and third, OPLANs 314 and 316, were for an invasion of Cuba. The constant improvement of these plans was a concern not only of the military experts involved but of the president himself.

Military planning for Cuba soon became linked to Operation Mongoose (named after the ferretlike Indian mammal capable of killing cobras), the secret campaign started by President Kennedy at the end of November 1961 "to use our available assets . . . to help Cuba overthrow the Communist regime." In handling international issues, JFK liked to give a particular individual the authority to coordinate the work of officials from a variety of government departments. He saw this as a way of energizing government bureaucracies, making sure they contributed to rather than stifled the creation of solutions to policy problems. In the case of Cuba, Kennedy selected General Edward Lansdale, a man viewed by many in Washington as a genius in the field of covert operations.

After entering the military in World War II, Lansdale became an air force officer. He ran anti-Communist campaigns in both the Philippines and Vietnam during the 1950s, efforts that enhanced his reputation. He was viewed as the quintessential spy, and even inspired Graham Greene's *The Quiet American*. At the close of the Eisenhower presidency Lansdale was working in "special operations." The Kennedy administration decided to retain Lansdale's services. His role, as he later explained, was to help "the Armed Forces get ready for counterinsurgency."

Apart from Lansdale, Robert Kennedy was the senior official most active in shaping Operation Mongoose. After the

Bay of Pigs disaster he took an active interest in foreign policy matters despite his position as attorney general. More than anyone else in the administration, he was determined to make amends for the humiliation at the Bay of Pigs; and in trying to weaken Castro he was highly attracted to covert techniques. It was thus no surprise that in the effort to launch Mongoose, Robert Kennedy played a central role. He would continue to do so during the implementation of the operation.

Mongoose received its initial direction at a meeting of senior officials in December 1961. At the start of this discussion Robert Kennedy informed his colleagues that the outcome of a number of recent meetings involving the president had been a decision that "higher priority should be given to Cuba." General Lansdale, he reported, was to be chief of operations for Mongoose. It was agreed that Lansdale would be asked to devise a long-term program for Cuba that should then be reviewed. In his remarks, Lansdale stressed that Mongoose's basic objective was one "of fomenting eventual revolution within Cuba" in order to overthrow Castro. He added that it was important to reach "an agreement at some early date as to the future of Cuba after the Castro government is overthrown, so that appeals to potential resistance elements can be geared to a positive long-range program." (The extent to which Mongoose planners assumed that direct American intervention would also be required became clear in the following weeks.)

In one key respect, Mongoose embraced the same flawed assumption that the Bay of Pigs operation had: that substantial, potentially overwhelming opposition to Castro existed in Cuba. Although that might have come to be the case in later years, it was not so in 1961–1962. The CIA's own evidence at the time indicated that. An agency memorandum, produced less than four weeks before the start of Mongoose, stated that

"The Castro regime has sufficient popular support and repressive capabilities to cope with any internal threat likely to develop within the foreseeable future." Despite the gap between Castro's promises and actual accomplishments, "The bulk of the population . . . still accepts the Castro regime, or is at least resigned to it, and substantial numbers still support it with enthusiasm."

In establishing Operation Mongoose, however, some lessons were learned from the Bay of Pigs. Mongoose was set up with clear lines of authority, and with the president, through the proxy of Robert Kennedy, maintaining a direct link to the planning process. Once Lansdale, who was based in the Pentagon, had developed a course of action, he was obliged to submit it for approval to the Special Group (Augmented) (SGA), the body ordinarily charged with overseeing covert operations but enlarged by the inclusion of Robert Kennedy and presidential military adviser General Maxwell Taylor. The SGA would then report to the president.

Complementing the policymaking component of Mongoose was the establishment of a CIA unit, Task Force W, responsible for implementing the policies. William Harvey headed up that unit. From the agency's headquarters at Langley, Virginia, he oversaw the activities of the Miami station, the CIA outpost centrally involved in Operation Mongoose.

From the start, Mongoose overseers adopted the military contingency planning for Cuba already in place. Their focus was on developing the conditions necessary for an anti-Castro revolt within Cuba; but they believed that American military intervention might be required to ensure the success of such an uprising. In the early days of Mongoose, Defense Department officials were asked to prepare "a contingency plan for U.S. military action, in case the Cuban people request U.S. help when their revolt starts making headway." This plan might have to be carried out, Lansdale believed, but even if it were not, its mere existence would be helpful because it would encourage anti-Castro Cubans.

On January 18, 1962, Lansdale produced a substantial memorandum defining Mongoose's fundamental purpose, recording the progress made thus far, and mapping out future developments. The aim, Lansdale again made clear, was "to help the Cubans overthrow the Communist regime from within Cuba and institute a new government with which the United States can live in peace." To promote the success of an anti-Castro movement, "economic warfare" would be carried out to make sure the present government was unable to meet its citizens' material expectations, and "psychological operations" would be used "to turn the peoples' resentment increasingly against the regime." Once an uprising against Castro had begun, the United States and perhaps other nations in the Western Hemisphere should be ready to "give open support to the Cuban peoples' revolt. Such support will include military force, as necessary."

In his assignments to government agencies, Lansdale instructed the Defense Department to formulate a contingency plan for the use of force against Cuba, and to outline the conditions that would make it necessary to implement that plan. The CIA was asked to come up with a schedule for sabotage operations against Cuba as well as an explanation of how those activities would serve to encourage an anti-Castro movement. The tasks given to the State Department related to the application of additional economic pressures against Cuba.

Lansdale promised in this memorandum to come up with "a firm time table" for Mongoose. True to his word, he did so on February 20 with a clear, bold, and uncompromising plan of action. Using 1776 as a reference point, Lansdale observed that "Americans once ran a successful revolution. It was run from within, and succeeded because there was timely and strong political, economic, and military help by nations outside who supported our cause. Using this same concept of revolution from within, we must now help the Cuban people to stamp out tyranny and gain their liberty." What France was to the American revolutionaries of the 1770s, the United States would be to anti-Castro Cubans in the 1960s. Lansdale presented a six-part plan for Mongoose, culminating in the overthrow of Castro in October 1962.

To Lansdale's dismay, Mongoose planners did not endorse his scheme. It was decided instead to make intelligence gathering the focus of the operation until the summer of 1962, although other, more explicitly anti-Castro activities were to be permitted. In the summer more ambitious objectives might be set.

President Kennedy was involved in this decision to limit Mongoose's initial mandate, but he also approved the idea that the United States should ultimately be prepared to use force to assist an anti-Castro uprising. This occurred when the SGA laid down its guidelines for the operation's first phase in mid-March. It agreed that in seeking the overthrow of Castro, Mongoose would make use of anti-Castro Cubans already on the island as well as Cuban refugees; and that the "final success [of the operation] will require decisive U.S. military intervention." These guidelines were discussed in Kennedy's presence and apparently received his tacit endorsement.

Despite its initial limitations, Mongoose was a substantial enterprise. The CIA station in Miami was greatly enlarged. Mongoose soon became the largest American covert operation in CIA history, exceeding even the level of organization established for the Bay of Pigs invasion. Among the resources devoted to Mongoose were four hundred CIA officers, an annual budget of probably more than $50 million, and a fleet of hundreds of motorboats in the Miami area and the Florida Keys.

Mongoose's first phase comprised three elements. In addition to collecting intelligence and improving contingency plans for military action against Cuba, "political, economic and covert actions" were, in the words of the SGA's own guidelines, to "be undertaken short of those reasonably calculated to inspire a revolt within the target area, or other development which would require U.S. armed intervention." These activities were to include acts of sabotage and psychological intimidation.

As part of the effort to gather more accurate intelligence, an attempt was made throughout the spring and summer of 1962 to infiltrate Cuban exiles back onto the island. Some of the teams failed to establish themselves, intercepted no doubt by the Castro regime; by May only three teams were in place. By midsummer, however, there were forty-five agents in the Havana area, according to Lansdale, and a number of others in the provinces.

American officials worked hard during Mongoose's first phase at developing contingency plans for military action against Cuba. In late March the Joint Chiefs of Staff (JCS) augmented the forces available under these plans, and in the same month a Caribbean order of battle was produced for Cuba, Haiti, and the Dominican Republic. In April the Defense Department studied the mechanics involved in blockading Cuba. Rumors of an anti-Castro uprising, according to Lansdale, prompted him to ask Defense for additional military planning.

Sabotage, economic coercion, and psychological intimidation, in addition to intelligence collection, were ongoing during the spring and summer. Deputy Secretary of Defense

Roswell Gilpatric has recalled in detail the effort put into these sorts of activities:

> ... The agency was allowed to put agents into Cuba for purposes of sabotage, for purposes of trying to disrupt the strengthening of the regime's control over areas that were not wholly committed to Castro. And the size of these efforts varied from teams of four or five individuals put in to sometimes several times that. And how they were put in, by air or by sea or by submarine or ship, and what the ground rules were and how to avoid the compromising, these things were all spelled out in great detail with just exactly the cost in terms of men and money, as well as the political consequences of a mission aborting, which they did many times. But there was, aside from the specific objective of destroying some installation or breaking some line of communication—taking a power plant or something like that—there was the more general objective of keeping the Castro [government] so off stride and unsettled that it couldn't concentrate its activities in harmful ends elsewhere. And so the agency, partly because they believed in these objectives and, I think, partly because they wanted to prove they could conduct this kind of activity effectively, was very aggressive in coming forward with schemes, some of which were really quite fantastic and never got off the ground. Others made a lot of sense, some of which did prove to be effective and successful.

Economic pressure was a focus for CIA officials, especially John McCone, appointed to replace Allen Dulles as director of the agency in late 1961, and for Deputy Director of Intelligence Ray Cline. Cline felt that the Cuban people would support or oppose Castro for economic rather than ideological reasons. If the Cuban leader provided them with an improved standard of living, he would be viewed as a success; if he did not, they would regard him as a failure. Consequently the CIA tried to damage the Cuban economy by trying "lots of little gimmicks like spoiling the bearings in certain kinds of machinery, putting flat bearings in instead of ball bearings, trying to adulterate petrol supplies with sugar and various contaminants." Opportunities to curtail Cuban trade with other nations were also explored. This sort of economic warfare apparently culminated in an August 1962 episode in which CIA agents broke into a Puerto Rican warehouse and, using a nontoxic substance, contaminated Cuban sugar bound for the Soviet Union.

Attempts at psychological intimidation during Mongoose's first phase were more limited. An interagency Cuba Psychological Operations Group and the United States Information Agency (which could use Voice of America radio broadcasts or the print media to disseminate information) were pressed into service. As Lansdale acknowledged, however, the Kennedy administration was unable to communicate reliably with the Cuban people. Most Cubans did not have shortwave radio receivers and so could not pick up these American propaganda broadcasts; and attempts at medium-frequency transmissions were usually blocked by more powerful Cuban signals. The idea of distributing propaganda leaflets throughout Cuba was raised, but the SGA had not approved the proposal.

While Mongoose was working to undermine Castro's position in Cuba, Washington was also seeking to contain his influence within the Western Hemisphere. During the early part of his presidency, JFK had bolstered the military and police in Latin American countries in order to help them meet "the internal Communist threat supported externally by Castro," as one American official put it. At the end of 1961 both the CIA and the JCS recommended the establishment of a group of senior officials to coordinate the various counterinsurgency efforts not only against Castro but against the left generally in the Third World. Accordingly Kennedy signed a policy directive in January 1962 to create just such a body, to be called the Special Group (Counter-Insurgency). Although distinct from the SGA, it included many of the same officials, including Robert Kennedy. The group was charged with ensuring "unity of effort and the use of all available resources with maximum effectiveness in preventing and resisting subversive insurgency and related forms of indirect aggression in friendly countries." More specifically, the Special Group (C.I.)'s responsibilities included promoting a general understanding of the importance of "subversive insurgency" and of "wars of national liberation" as threats to American interests. It was to make sure the military and other branches of government were ready to meet the challenge posed by this brand of warfare. Among actions taken under the rubric of counterinsurgency were the creation of a police academy for Latin American students and the establishment of a seminar series at the Foreign Service Institute, "Problems of Development and Internal Defense," which Kennedy expected important military and civilian officials to attend.

On July 25, 1962, Lansdale reported to the SGA on the progress made during Phase I of Operation Mongoose. While generally upbeat, he pleaded for more help for anti-Castro Cubans. "Assets among the Cubans, to liberate themselves, are capable of a greater effectiveness," he argued, "once a firm decision is made by the U.S. to provide maximum support of Cubans to liberate Cuba, and the Cubans start being helped towards that goal by the U.S." Lansdale wanted a more aggressive second phase of Mongoose, with a greater willingness to use American resources, military and otherwise, to ensure the operation's success. His more ambitious approach was vigorously debated among senior foreign policy officials.

Operation Mongoose was not the only covert approach used by the Kennedy administration to weaken Castro. A more ethically troubling but potentially decisive technique was that of assassination, often referred to euphemistically in government circles as "executive action." As with the Bay of Pigs and the contingencies for military action against Cuba, the planning for Castro's assassination preceded Kennedy's inauguration as president, originating in a cluster of schemes devised during the spring and summer of 1960. These included spraying the studio Castro used for broadcasts with a chemical that had similar effects to LSD and so might impair the Cuban leader's speech; or dusting thallium salts on Castro's shoes to make his beard drop out, thereby destroying his image as "The Beard." These and other imaginative schemes fell through.

In the early days of the Kennedy presidency, just before the Bay of Pigs operation, the CIA made at least one attempt—perhaps two—to kill Castro. This plot involved the recruitment of mobsters John Rosselli, Sam Giancana, head of the Chicago Mafia, and Santos Trafficante, the Cosa Nostra chief in Cuba. Either Rosselli or Giancana suggested poisoning Castro's drink with a substance that would later disappear without a trace. The CIA's Technical Services Division prepared the pills, which a Cuban passed on to an official in Castro's government sometime just before the Bay of Pigs invasion. The plan failed for reasons that are unclear.

There appears to have been a second attempt on Castro's life before the Bay of Pigs, this plot involving a Cuban exile whom Trafficante felt was capable of organizing the assassination. The exile claimed to know someone who worked in one of Castro's favorite restaurants, and the plan was for him to deliver poison pills to his restaurant contact who would then put them in Castro's food. As with all the plots, this one fizzled out.

In late 1961, control of the effort to assassinate Castro passed to William Harvey, a CIA official whom Lansdale once described to President Kennedy as America's James Bond. In the spring of 1962 Harvey met Rosselli in Miami, asking him to continue cultivating his Cuban contacts. During another Miami discussion in late April, Harvey gave Rosselli four poison pills. "These would work anywhere," he assured the mobster, "and at any time with anything." Rosselli indicated to Harvey that the pills would be used to eliminate Castro adviser Ernesto Che Guevara and Raúl Castro, as well as Fidel.

By May 1962 Rosselli was able to report to Harvey that the pills and some guns were in Cuba. Then, toward the end of June, he informed Harvey that a three-man team had been sent to the island—their mission to use the poison pills to assassinate Castro or to pass them to others who could bring it off, should the opportunity arise. Plainly, it never did. In September Harvey received news that the pills were still in Cuba. There was talk of dispatching a second three-man team, but the mission never materialized.

Much of this information on the CIA effort to kill Castro was revealed during a 1975 Senate investigation into alleged assassination attempts on foreign leaders. An issue that concerned the senators was whether these efforts were made with presidential approval or on the CIA's own initiative.

It is virtually certain that President Kennedy was aware of CIA plans to kill Castro, and it is probable that he gave them his tacit or explicit endorsement. On at least two occasions he discussed the possibility of assassinating Castro—once with a senator who was also a close friend, and once with a journalist.

According to the reporter's notes of that meeting, Kennedy said "he was under terrific pressure from advisers (think he said intelligence people, but not positive) to okay a Castro murder." Unless he ordered the CIA to scrap its plans to eliminate Castro and the CIA simply ignored him, Kennedy must have approved the assassination attempts, for they were ongoing throughout his presidency.

The assassination plots, together with Operation Mongoose and the military contingency plans for Cuba, made for a powerful and covert drive to oust Castro. In the public domain, policies designed to weaken the Cuban leader's position or at least intimidate him complemented the clandestine initiatives. Using diplomatic channels, the Kennedy administration sought to isolate Castro from other nations in the Western Hemisphere. A little more than a week into his presidency, JFK asked the State Department to develop a strategy to bring about a condemnation of the Cuban government in the Organization of American States (OAS). The clumsy Bay of Pigs invasion outraged many Latin American states, making that plan more difficult to implement. Dispatching his UN ambassador, Adlai Stevenson, on a goodwill mission to South America in the early summer of 1961 allowed Kennedy to pour oil on those troubled waters. The administration's effort to bring diplomatic pressure to bear on Castro culminated in the OAS decision in early 1962, at the conference held in Punta del Este, Uruguay, to expel Cuba.

Economic as well as diplomatic pressure was another feature of JFK's public approach to the Cuban problem. Only a few weeks into his presidency, he asked the State Department to consider extending Eisenhower's ban on exports to Cuba to those goods still imported from the island, such as tobacco and molasses. That policy, Rusk was able to confirm, would indeed damage the Cuban economy. A year later Kennedy and Rusk felt the time for the economic embargo was ripe, and on February 7, 1962, it was ordered. No Cuban-American trade was now permitted, save for the export of vital foodstuffs and medical supplies to Cuba.

Later in the spring of 1962 Kennedy authorized a number of military maneuvers in the Caribbean. Generating considerable publicity, including several substantial *New York Times* articles, these seemed designed not only to test the feasibility of existing military plans but to remind Castro and his chief ally, the Soviet Union, of America's determination to stay firmly in control of its own backyard. The first of these practice operations involved a force some forty thousand strong and concluded with a landing on Vieques, an island near Puerto Rico.

The Kennedy administration's policies toward Cuba to the spring of 1962 were thus marked by an unremitting hostility. In authorizing an invasion by Cuban emigrés, initiating Operation Mongoose, developing military contingency plans, attempting to assassinate the Cuban leader, applying diplomatic and economic pressure, and staging large-scale military maneuvers, the Kennedy administration tried everything short of a direct attack by American forces to displace Castro. These policies could scarcely help but influence the decision made by Khrushchev and accepted by Castro to put nuclear missiles in Cuba.

2

The Soviets Act: Operation Anadyr

WHY DID NIKITA Khrushchev decide in the spring of 1962 to install nuclear weapons in Cuba? That question has remained the greatest enigma among the many that punctuate the history of the missile crisis. Making sense of Khrushchev's gamble has been difficult partly because his foreign policy in general has defied understanding. Impulsive, moody, and unpredictable, Khrushchev, who had emerged by the mid-1950s as the successor to Joseph Stalin, approached international affairs in a way that seemed to mirror his own personality. On the one hand, the Soviet leader pursued the idea of "peaceful coexistence" with the West, made the sort of sweeping military cuts that no American president dared carry out during the cold war, and agreed to the withdrawal of Soviet troops from Austria. On the other hand, he set up the Warsaw Pact (a military alliance between the Soviet Union and its Eastern European satellite states), crushed the 1956 Hungarian uprising, threatened to inflict nuclear annihilation on other countries with reckless abandon, and provoked crises, such as those in Berlin in 1958–1959 and 1961, that moved the world to the brink of war. At his best, Khrushchev was more innovative and conciliatory than any other Soviet or American leader before Mikhail Gorbachev. At his worst, he was more erratic and dangerous.

Khrushchev gave his own explanation of why he put nuclear weapons in Cuba only a few weeks after the missile crisis had ended. "Our purpose," he declared in a December 1962 speech,

> was only the defense of Cuba. Everybody saw how the American imperialists were sharpening the knives and threatening Cuba with a massed attack. . . . We saw a possibility of defending the freedom-loving people of Cuba by stationing missiles there. . . . We were confident that this step would bring the aggressors to their senses and that they, realizing that Cuba was not defenseless and American imperialism not omnipotent, would be obliged to change their plans.

In the memoirs he recorded after being ousted from power in 1964, Khrushchev, though mentioning several factors, once again claimed that his main objective had been to defend Cuba by deterring an inevitable American assault.

For two decades or more, most Western observers treated Khrushchev's explanation with skepticism. It seemed self-serving of him to say that his decision to deploy missiles was unrelated to any selfish Soviet concerns, such as the desire to increase the number of nuclear weapons capable of striking American territory. Beginning in the late 1980s, however, former Soviet officials offered their recollections of events for the first time, and their arguments often echoed Khrushchev's. Sergo Mikoyan (son of Anastas Mikoyan, probably Khrushchev's closest adviser in 1962), Andrei Gromyko, and former Khrushchev aide Oleg Troyanovsky have all stated that the Soviet premier's chief motive was the defense of Cuba.

In calculating that the United States was poised to attack Cuba, Khrushchev and his advisers believed the evidence to be overwhelming. Of all the reasons why the Soviet leadership thought an assault was imminent, the most frequently cited

was the simple fact that Kennedy had authorized the Bay of
Pigs invasion. That plainly showed he was prepared to use
force to overthrow Castro; and Khrushchev's logic was that if
JFK had ordered military action to topple the Cuban leader
once, there was no reason to think he would not do so again,
perhaps once more using Cuban exiles but also employing
American troops to make sure the attack succeeded. As Khrushchev put it, "We were quite certain that the [Bay of Pigs] invasion was only the beginning and that the Americans would
not let Cuba alone."

The secret aspects of Kennedy's Cuban policies in 1961 and
1962 probably also convinced the Soviets that Kennedy was
desperate to be rid of Castro and that a U.S. attack on Cuba
was thus likely. The extent to which Moscow knew about Operation Mongoose and the assassination attempts is not altogether clear, but the evidence suggests that Khrushchev and
his advisers did receive information about these covert operations.

The nature of Mongoose, if not the name itself, was almost
certainly known in Moscow. Cuban officials have confirmed
that their agents had infiltrated the sabotage teams used in the
operation. "We knew there was a plan involving certain actions against Cuba, which was Operation Mongoose," a
Cuban official has revealed. "We found out about that code-
name afterwards." Given that Castro had a vested interest in
presenting as much evidence as possible to the Soviets about
the threat posed by the United States, this sort of information
must surely have been passed on to Moscow.

Soviet knowledge of the CIA's attempts on Castro's life is
difficult to establish. A few pieces of evidence indicate that at
the very least Soviet (and Cuban) officials suspected that assassination plots were being devised. In the UN General Assembly in the fall of 1961, the Cuban representative charged the

Kennedy administration with planning the elimination of his country's political leaders. Ambassador Stevenson, who was probably unaware of the assassination plans, categorically rejected the claim. Soviet officials nonetheless picked up the issue. Eighteen days later the Soviet publication *Komsomolskaya pravda* printed an article alleging that the United States was organizing courses in Buenos Aires designed "to train cadres of provocateurs and assassins for all Latin American countries, [but] primarily, of course, for actions against Cuba."

Even had Khrushchev ignored American covert operations and planning against Cuba on the grounds that the evidence was not reliable, he would still have been struck by the Kennedy administration's growing hostility toward Castro as indicated by its public actions in early 1962. The removal of Cuba from the OAS had a decided impact on Soviet perceptions. According to Sergo Mikoyan, the Soviet premier regarded this as nothing less than "a diplomatic isolation and a preparation for an invasion." Kennedy's economic sanctions no doubt magnified those suspicions.

U.S. military maneuvers in the Caribbean strengthened the Soviet belief that Kennedy was about to attack Cuba. Anatoly Gribkov, a central figure in the operation to deploy Soviet troops, missiles, and conventional weapons in Cuba, has disclosed that in the spring of 1962 Khrushchev received "a spate of intelligence reports of U.S. plans for a second invasion" of Cuba. These must have related to the military maneuvers in the Caribbean.

Looking at the situation from Khrushchev's perspective in April 1962, the evidence that Kennedy was poised to authorize an attack on Cuba seemed very strong. The Bay of Pigs invasion had clearly demonstrated JFK's determination to remove Castro and his willingness to use force to bring that about. Cuban expulsion from the OAS and the sanctions that followed appeared to represent the diplomatic and economic preludes to an assault, while the military maneuvers in the Caribbean were not unreasonably interpreted in Moscow as dry runs for a real attack. The information Khrushchev probably received on Operation Mongoose and the assassination plots would only have added to his sense that Kennedy was ready to attack Cuba. If Khrushchev decided to place missiles in Cuba partly in order to deter JFK from carrying out military action, it can only be said that Kennedy's policies toward Castro in 1961 and 1962, not the Soviet leader's exaggerated fears, were largely responsible for Khrushchev's perception of the situation.

Although several scholars of the missile crisis are attracted to the defend-Cuba theory as an explanation for the Soviet missile deployment, that argument requires elaboration if it is to be convincing. To maintain that Khrushchev installed missiles in Cuba primarily because he wished to protect the island from an anticipated American attack does not in itself identify the Soviet interests involved. The question that must be asked is, What did Khrushchev have to gain by defending Cuba with nuclear weapons?

There are a number of possible answers. Sustaining a friendly government anywhere in the world meant one more ally for Moscow, one less for Washington, in the ongoing cold war. Keeping Castro in power also provided a dynamic socialist model for other Latin American countries. Perhaps most important, defending Castro helped Khrushchev with what by the spring of 1962 was one of his highest priorities—meeting the challenge that China, the second most powerful Communist nation, had mounted to Soviet leadership of the world Communist movement.

Khrushchev's talk of the need for peaceful coexistence between East and West had been seized upon by the Chinese to portray him as "soft" and to argue that he was too reluctant to back revolutionary movements, such as Castro's in Cuba. Khrushchev was fully aware that the objective behind this Chinese attack was nothing less than the replacement of Soviet leadership of world communism with a Chinese alternative. From this point of view, a bold, dramatic initiative, such as an attempt to protect Cuba with a nuclear umbrella, would aid Khrushchev in the politics of world communism. It would enable him to rebut the Chinese argument that he was ineffective in bolstering socialism across the globe.

Khrushchev may also have regarded the missile deployment as a way to help correct the imbalance between the Soviet and American nuclear arsenals. Sparked by the Soviet development of Sputnik and the world's first ICBM, both in 1957, the idea that Moscow was winning the arms race became commonly accepted in the United States. The strategic reality was very different. Not until the 1970s did the Soviet Union achieve anything close to missile parity with the United States. At the time Khrushchev decided to place missiles in Cuba, American missile superiority over the Soviet Union was vast. Recent estimates on the extent of the gap vary from a 17-to-1 to a 9-to-1 U.S. advantage in nuclear warheads. Whatever the case, the disparity was enormous. And the Soviets knew it. Sergo Mikoyan has acknowledged that at the start of the 1960s "U.S. superiority was well known" in Moscow.

Not only did the Soviet-American nuclear gap trouble Khrushchev, but also the way the Kennedy administration exploited it. Where Eisenhower had not spoken publicly about the strategic lead enjoyed by the United States, officials in the Kennedy administration displayed no such reluctance. Beginning in the fall of 1961 they spoke openly of American strategic superiority. Soon the talk even shifted to the possibility that this advantage could be used to launch a first-strike attack on the Soviet Union, destroying its nuclear missiles aimed at the United States before those weapons could be fired in retaliation. Remarkably, Kennedy said as much in a March 1962 interview. JFK's comments caused considerable concern in Moscow. *Pravda* denounced Kennedy's suggestions, and the Soviet leadership ordered a special military alert. It may have been more than coincidence that Khrushchev appears to have hatched the plan to place missiles in Cuba only a few weeks after JFK had declared that a first-strike on the Soviet Union should be regarded as a policy option.

Although it was almost certainly not his sole motive, it is clear that altering the nuclear equation by increasing the number of missiles capable of reaching the United States was an important consideration for Khrushchev. In his memoirs he offers the defend-Cuba theory as the main explanation, but he does discuss the strategic issue. Some Soviet officials, such as Khrushchev's speechwriter Fedor Burlatsky, have confirmed that this was indeed a key factor behind the missile deployment.

As well as being an end in itself, the improved strategic situation brought about by nuclear weapons in Cuba might bring the Soviets additional benefits. First, it could help Khrushchev achieve his deeply held objective of reducing military spending and putting the resources thus saved into the civilian economy. Knowing that more of his defense budget went to conventional forces than to nuclear weaponry; regarding the latter as far more important militarily; and believing he must try to raise the general standard of living in the Soviet Union, Khrushchev calculated that he could simultaneously modernize his nuclear arsenal, cut spending on conventional forces, trim overall defense expenditures, and invest the savings in the civilian economy.

During the late 1950s he pursued that goal with some success. Soviet troop numbers, for instance, were reduced from more than 5.7 million in 1955 to just over 3.6 million by 1959. Capping his drive to prune the military was Khrushchev's announcement in January 1960 that military personnel would be further cut by no less than a third. But when he was faced with a large U.S. military buildup initiated by Kennedy early in his presidency, and opposition to cuts within his own military, Khrushchev reluctantly announced in July 1961 that the planned reduction would have to be postponed.

Placing missiles in Cuba might therefore have been viewed by Khrushchev as a way of resuming his program of military cuts. Nuclear weapons in the Caribbean would in effect give the Soviet Union a new group of ICBMs that could strike the American mainland. Khrushchev could make that point to his military advisers, arguing that weapons in Cuba equalized the increases in American defense spending; hence it would be safe to continue with the cuts he had announced in January 1960.

Khrushchev's missile gambit in Cuba may also have been a feature of the brinkmanship he liked to use as a diplomatic instrument. That strategy is associated with John Foster Dulles, Eisenhower's secretary of state, who believed it was sometimes necessary to threaten cold war adversaries with nuclear destruction in order to make them comply with American objectives. Khrushchev employed brinkmanship as well, appearing to view it as a cost-efficient tactic. Foreign policy goals could be secured through rhetorical blustering rather than by expending precious resources or taking risky military action.

What made Khrushchev's brinkmanship feasible in the late 1950s was Eisenhower's refusal to use the intelligence data at his disposal to show the American people and the international community that the United States enjoyed a vast strategic superiority over the Soviet Union. Eisenhower appears to have calculated that this revelation would only embarrass Khrushchev and impel him to increase Soviet defense spending. This would force Washington to respond in kind, thereby making a balanced budget (a key policy objective for conservative Republicans) even more difficult.

Kennedy, by contrast, had no wish to hide the extent of the American lead in nuclear weapons. In October 1961 his close aide Roswell Gilpatric explained that rather than losing the arms race, as many Americans assumed to be the case in the late 1950s, the United States was in fact winning it hands down. This revelation meant that Khrushchev's brinkmanship, based as it had been on the idea that the Soviets were second-to-none in nuclear weapons, was no longer credible. That being the case, Khrushchev might well have hoped that the threat to the United States of a missile deployment in the Caribbean would allow him to indulge his taste for nuclear brinkmanship once more. As he later said about the installation of missiles in Cuba, "We saw that our weapons could inspire terror."

A final motive behind Khrushchev's placement of missiles in Cuba may have been a desire to improve his hand in the ongoing dispute over Berlin. Since 1958 the Soviet premier had been trying desperately to remove the Western powers from that city which lay deep within the territory of East Germany, a Soviet satellite. In the process Khrushchev had provoked two crises, the first during the Eisenhower years in 1958–1959 and the second in 1961. But he failed to remove the Western powers from Berlin, though he did order the building of the Berlin Wall to prevent East Germans from fleeing to the West. Perhaps the Soviet leader hoped that missiles in Cuba would change the Berlin equation, compelling Kennedy to be more conciliatory over this issue. According to Dean Rusk, a

"top-ranking Russian" dropped a hint after the missile crisis
that the Soviets had intended to "use the Cuban missiles as additional leverage with us on Berlin." Some former Soviet officials have indicated that Khrushchev did indeed think in terms
of such a linkage between the Berlin and Cuban situations.

In understanding Khrushchev's decision to deploy nuclear
weapons in Cuba, two other issues, apart from the question of
motive, need to be considered. First, why did he think he was
justified? At some point the presence of missiles in Cuba was
certain to become known, obliging him to defend his action
before the international community. Second, why did Khrushchev think Kennedy would allow him to install nuclear
weapons just off the coast of Florida without retaliating militarily?

Khrushchev believed the presence of American Jupiter
missiles in Italy and especially those on the Soviet border in
Turkey justified his deployment of missiles in Cuba, even
though these American weapons were practically obsolete.
Aleksandr Alekseyev, the man appointed Soviet ambassador
to Cuba in the spring of 1962, recalls Khrushchev feeling that
"we had every right to do it because Turkey had missiles, Italy
had missiles." Sergo Mikoyan has explained that Khrushchev
intended to inform Kennedy of the weapons in Cuba after the
November congressional elections, and "he expected it would
be received in the United States as the Turkish missiles were
received in the Soviet Union."

As to why Khrushchev believed he could put nuclear
weapons in Cuba without risking American retaliation, perhaps he felt JFK would have no alternative but to accept a *fait
accompli*, assuming the United States did not find out about
the missile deployment until it was complete. The Soviet
leader's perception of JFK could also have shaped his thinking. After the two men met in Vienna in June 1961, the con-

ventional wisdom for many years thereafter was that Khrushchev went away feeling that JFK was a weak leader. Some recollections reinforce this view. One former official has said that Khrushchev got the impression Kennedy was "very young, too intellectual, not strong enough to handle" and "not prepared well for decision making in crisis situations." On the other hand, Khrushchev's son, Sergei, has written that "Father returned to Moscow after the summit with a very high opinion of Kennedy. He saw him as a worthy partner and a strong statesman."

Even if Khrushchev did acquire an unflattering view of JFK in Vienna, it seems likely that Kennedy's tough, unyielding performance during the crisis over Berlin later that summer, and his talk in the spring of 1962 of the possible need for a first strike against the Soviet Union, would have altered that perception. Given the conflicting evidence on this question, the prudent conclusion is that Khrushchev *might* have thought Kennedy would not react vigorously to a missile deployment in Cuba because of the evaluation he had made at Vienna—and perhaps during the Bay of Pigs fiasco as well.

All these considerations—his objectives, his justifications, and possibly his appraisal of Kennedy as president—resulted in Khrushchev's decision to install nuclear weapons in Cuba. The spark for the idea seems to have come from a conversation he had with Defense Minister Rodion Malinovsky in the Crimea. As the two men were strolling along the Black Sea coast, Malinovsky observed that American missiles based just over the horizon in Turkey could strike Soviet cities in only a few minutes. Khrushchev responded that if Soviet missiles were located in Cuba, they would place the United States under a similar threat. He also implied that Kennedy would not be able to complain about it because American leaders had not asked for Soviet approval before deploying their weapons in Turkey.

Having raised the possibility of missiles in Cuba for the first time, Khrushchev took up the idea with Anastas Mikoyan, his close adviser, good friend, and Cuba expert. After Khrushchev explained his interest in secretly installing missiles in Cuba and then revealing this to the world after the U.S. congressional elections in November, Mikoyan pointed out problems with the plan. Castro, he predicted, would not go along with it because the missile deployment might lead to an American invasion. Anyway, American intelligence was sure to detect the operation.

Not discouraged by these warnings, Khrushchev put the plan to a larger group of officials. During this meeting Mikoyan raised the same objections he had made privately: Castro would not cooperate, and the Americans would soon discover the operation. The Soviet leader, however, offered simple solutions to these problems: he would ask Castro if the plan was acceptable, and he would instruct his commander-in-chief of strategic missile forces, Sergei Biryuzov, to head a secret mission to Cuba to decide whether missiles could be deployed on the island without detection by the United States. Collectively the group endorsed Khrushchev's recommendations.

Discussions of the missile plan continued behind closed doors in the Kremlin during the spring. In early May another meeting of the same advisers convened, with the addition of Sharaf Rashidov and Aleksandr Alekseyev, whom Khrushchev had appointed only a few days earlier as Soviet ambassador to Cuba. Alekseyev now played the role of dissenter, as Mikoyan had earlier. When Khrushchev asked Alekseyev, who already knew Castro well, how the Cuban leader would react to the idea of missiles on his island, the new ambassador predicted that Castro would "not accept such a proposal from us, because he is building his security on, first, strengthening their defense capability, and [second] public opinion in Latin America and world public opinion." Khrushchev retorted that he still preferred nuclear missiles in Cuba as a deterrent against an American attack, but if Castro refused to accept them he would use all other military means to bolster the island's defenses. Again he declared his intention to send to Cuba a team that included Biryuzov and also Rashidov.

The plan to place missiles in Cuba, raising as it did a variety of military and diplomatic issues, touched more directly on the policy concerns of Defense Minister Malinovsky and Foreign Minister Andrei Gromyko than those of other Soviet officials. Where the defense minister strongly favored the missile deployment, Gromyko was more skeptical. When Khrushchev broached the matter with him in private, he found Gromyko less than enthusiastic. "It will cause a political explosion in the USA," he warned. "That has to be taken into account." From the nature of his later decisions, it is clear that Khrushchev, as in his dealings with Mikoyan and Alekseyev, failed to consider the doubts expressed by Gromyko.

The discussions between Khrushchev and his close advisers came to a halt for a week in mid-May 1962 when the Soviet leader embarked on a trip to Bulgaria. Although his time there was filled with speeches and political meetings, the question of Cuba dominated his thoughts. As Khrushchev later recalled, he kept asking himself: "What will happen if we lose Cuba? I knew it would have been a terrible blow to Marxism-Leninism. It would gravely diminish our stature throughout the world, but especially in Latin America." On May 20 Khrushchev returned to Moscow determined to put his plan into action.

The next day he met with the Defense Council, a body that

convened when there was a need for direct talks between political leaders in the Kremlin and senior military officials. A provisional decision was made on this occasion to deploy missiles in Cuba. In developing the case for this operation, Khrushchev asked Malinovsky to calculate the length of time it would take for his armed forces to seize control of a hypothetical island ninety miles from the Soviet coast. "Three to five days," Malinovsky estimated. "No more than a week." Cuba, Khrushchev commented, was equally vulnerable to an American attack. Installing missiles on the island, he asserted, was the only way to prevent such an assault.

The result of the meeting was a decision to place in Cuba missiles capable of delivering nuclear warheads to points across the United States. Soviet troops would be deployed as well to defend not only the island from American attack but the missile bases as well. This directive was only preliminary. Before the idea could be broached with Castro, a concrete operational plan would have to be drafted and then approved by both the Defense Council and the Presidium. Accordingly, Ministry of Defense officials produced a plan of action for presentation to Khrushchev and a joint session of the Defense Council and Presidium on May 24.

At that meeting Malinovsky outlined the plan that the Ministry of Defense had prepared. Khrushchev then added some remarks about Operation Anadyr, the name given to his proposed venture. According to the minutes taken at the time, "It was resolved to approve the ANADYR action wholly and unanimously." Officials also agreed to send to Cuba the Rashidov-Biryuzov mission. Although a solid phalanx of officials appeared to back Anadyr at this meeting, some evidence subtly suggests otherwise. For instance, the party secretaries in attendance failed to sign the minutes describing the meeting's decisions, as was customary. Khrushchev was unmoved on learning about this. "Not to worry," he said, "go around to their dachas. They'll sign." And they did.

Lack of unanimous support among senior officials for Operation Anadyr was also evident in a conversation between the Soviet leader and Troyanovsky, his close foreign policy aide, early in June. After Troyanovsky listed what he saw as weaknesses in the plan, Khrushchev explained why his decision was a reasonable one. The United States had already encircled the Soviet Union with nuclear missiles, he pointed out, so there was nothing unprecedented about Anadyr in terms of superpower behavior. In addition, the Monroe Doctrine, calling on European powers to stay out of the Western Hemisphere, and vice versa, no longer applied because the United States had been intervening in European affairs for a long time. Khrushchev's arguments were convincing, and Troyanovsky was unable to refute them. Still, the Soviet leader had failed to take into account the likely American reaction to his missile gambit.

In his memoirs Khrushchev suggests that the decision to move ahead with Operation Anadyr was made collaboratively and supported unanimously by senior Soviet officials. The reality was that Khrushchev hatched the plan and, though allowing an airing of the problems involved in executing it, then refused to allow the sort of vigorous internal debate that might have allowed dissenting views to prevail. Mikoyan, Alekseyev, Gromyko, and Troyanovsky had urged Khrushchev to be more cautious. To each of them the Soviet leader had responded by rationalizing his decision rather than by reconsidering the overall soundness of his plan. Just as Kennedy refused to be swayed by the opposition within his administration to the Bay of Pigs, so Khrushchev ignored the sensible advice offered by a variety of officials who felt less than enthusiastic about Operation Anadyr.

Even before the Rashidov-Biryuzov mission had returned from Cuba with its report, Khrushchev was buoyed by the idea of installing missiles just off the Florida coast. In a June 3, 1962, speech to a group of young Soviet and Cuban citizens, one overlooked by historians, Khrushchev promised to help Castro resist American pressure. "We are doing something to help Cuba," he declared, "with arms and other things."

It was the main purpose of the Rashidov-Biryuzov mission, ostensibly an agricultural delegation, to see whether Castro would accept those "other things" on his island. Biryuzov explored the local terrain, concluding that missiles could be deployed without attracting the attention of American intelligence. Meanwhile the proposal was put to Castro. This is an important element in the history of the missile crisis, for without Castro's approval of Operation Anadyr there would have been no nuclear confrontation in October 1962. Traditionally the missile crisis, both its origins and the event itself, has been viewed as an episode in the Soviet-American cold war. From that perspective, the deployment of nuclear weapons in the Caribbean was a Soviet decision with no important Cuban input, an idea based on the false assumption that Cuba was a Soviet satellite compelled to accept any initiative from Moscow. Recently various scholars, such as Philip Brenner, have argued for a triangular history of the missile crisis, three sides to the story: Soviet, American, and Cuban. It can be reasonably concluded, even after the incorporation of the Cuban element into the history of the missile crisis, that of the three powers involved, Cuba had by far the least influence over the course of events. Nevertheless the Cuban angle must be considered in writing the history of an event that American scholars do, after all, refer to as the *Cuban* missile crisis.

Khrushchev himself was aware that Cuba had a significant role to play. When he decided to put missiles on the island, he knew he would first need to win Castro's approval. In the May 24 meeting of the Defense Council and Presidium it was agreed that the plan for Operation Anadyr could only "be confirmed after obtaining consent from F. Castro." Khrushchev later acknowledged that he had been aware of the need to persuade Castro to accept the plan before being able to put it into effect.

When the "agricultural" delegation arrived in Cuba, Biryuzov briefed Castro about Operation Anadyr, stressing the importance of the missiles as a deterrent against an American invasion. Castro expressed support for the Soviet proposal but said he would have to counsel with his advisers. Rather than highlighting the importance of the missiles to Cuban security, however, he emphasized their value to the position of the socialist bloc in general. Castro did bring the Soviet proposal to the attention of his close advisers, a group that included Che Guevara, Emilio Aragonés, and Raúl Castro. To a man, they backed the plan. Fidel then told his Soviet guests that Operation Anadyr could proceed.

As with the question of Soviet motivation, the issue of why Castro and his advisers agreed to accept nuclear missiles in Cuba is controversial. Castro's own explanation for this has fluctuated over the years. On one occasion in 1963 he stated that "Cuba saw a danger to its security, and with an absolute right . . . adopted the measures that would fortify its defense." But in the same year he insisted that the aim was "not to assure our own defense, but first to reinforce socialism at an international level." Castro tried to clarify matters in 1992 by saying the decision to accept the Soviet offer was grounded in both considerations—the desire to help the socialist bloc and to bolster Cuban security—but of the two, the former was most important. Nuclear weapons might give the impression that Cuba was being turned into a Soviet military base, Castro argued, and that might damage the image of the Cuban revolution throughout Latin America. Moreover, he did not believe the missiles were needed to defend the island. Hence the desire to help world socialism was the primary objective, the defense of Cuba only the second.

Despite Castro's assertion, probably his chief aim was to deter an attack from the United States. All the developments that had worried Khrushchev—the Bay of Pigs, America's economic embargo, the ejection of Cuba from the OAS, Mongoose, the spring 1962 military maneuvers in the Caribbean—concerned Castro to an even greater degree because they threatened the security of *his* country.

At a June 10 meeting of the Presidium and Defense Council, Biryuzov and Rashidov reported on their mission to Cuba. Both Rashidov's account of Castro's response and Biryuzov's assessment of the feasibility of secretly deploying missiles in Cuba were highly positive. Following these reports, Malinovsky read out a memorandum that provided a more elaborate version of the May 24 Ministry of Defense plan. The minutes for the June 10 meeting record that "everyone voted in favor [of it]." By mid-June the dissenting voices heard in May had become inaudible.

The next stage in defining Anadyr came in early July when Raúl Castro visited Moscow for discussions with Malinovsky and Khrushchev on the precise arrangements to be made for the deployment of Soviet missiles, conventional weapons, and troops in Cuba. The draft of a five-year treaty formalizing the Soviet-Cuban agreement was produced by Soviet officials at this time and then approved by Malinovsky and Raúl Castro.

The question of whether Khrushchev would ultimately sign this formal agreement, which was tied to the broader issue of whether Moscow and Havana should publicize the plan to put missiles in Cuba even before the deployment was complete, came to divide Fidel Castro and Khrushchev during the late summer of 1962. After the draft agreement was approved in Moscow, Ambassador Alekseyev showed it to Castro, who made several amendments. Che Guevara and Aragonés carried Castro's updated version of the accord back to the Soviet Union in late August.

That draft agreement stated that Soviet military aid was aimed at providing protection for Cuba "in the event of [American] aggression," a provision that can be used to support the defend-Cuba argument as an explanation for the motives of both Khrushchev and Castro. Interestingly, this document also refers to Soviet security concerns. "The urgency of taking measures to assure *mutual defense* in the face of possible aggression against the Republic of Cuba *and the USSR* [my emphases]" reflected Moscow's fears that Kennedy might be tempted to launch a preemptive nuclear strike on the Soviet Union.

Despite the insistence of Che Guevara and Aragonés in August, Khrushchev refused to sign the pact—at least not until November, by which time the missiles would be in place. (A communiqué on the general military aid being supplied to Cuba was released in early September, however). The Cubans, for their part, believed that signing the agreement and then releasing it publicly would make it more difficult for Kennedy to respond militarily than if American intelligence were to detect a secret operation before the nuclear weapons were ready to fire. Khrushchev, though, was confident the United States would not learn about the missiles before they were in place, and that is what he told Aragonés and Che Guevara during their discussion. When they pressed him on what he would do if the missiles were discovered, the Soviet leader said he would defend Cuba by sending the Baltic fleet to the Caribbean and then dispatching a letter to Kennedy explaining his course of action.

Unlike Castro and his advisers, Khrushchev seems to have believed that even with the signing and public release of a formal agreement, Kennedy would not have tolerated missiles in Cuba. The problem with installing missiles secretly, however, was that if detected they would suggest something sinister and threatening to U.S. interests. Announcing the plan to put missiles in Cuba beforehand might have created an altogether different impression, a sense that the operation was aboveboard. Consequently it may have been more difficult for Kennedy from a political and public relations perspective to have taken the sort of forceful action that he ultimately did during the missile crisis. A few advisers who were close to JFK have lent their support to this theory. According to Theodore Sorensen, a publicly announced missile deployment in Cuba would have made it "much more difficult [for Kennedy] to mobilize world opinion on his side," a judgment in which McGeorge Bundy concurs.

The argument is convincing. In Khrushchev's defense, it can be said his miscalculation was entirely understandable. By the nature of his actions in 1961 and 1962, Kennedy had made clear that he did not accept the mere existence of Castro's government in Cuba. It was thus reasonable, if mistaken, for Khrushchev to believe that a Castro government publicly promised nuclear weapons from the Soviet Union would have prompted JFK to take military action.

The end result of Khrushchev's approval of Operation Anadyr, the secret deliberations of his military advisers, and the dialogue between them and their Cuban counterparts was a multifaceted military buildup on the Caribbean island. Nuclear weaponry was only one component of a deployment that would include almost 42,000 Soviet troops and such conventional equipment as surface-to-air missiles and IL-28 light bombers. The nuclear arsenal to be established in Cuba was to consist of twenty-four SS-4 medium-range ballistic missiles (MRBMs) and sixteen SS-5 intermediate-range ballistic missiles (IRBMs) and warheads, with a number of additional MRBM and IRBM missiles to be held in reserve as replacements for any weapons with technical faults; three short-range Luna units with a total of twelve missiles and warheads; and (though this is a recent revelation that not all missile crisis scholars would accept) probably eighty tactical cruise missiles and six IL-28 bombers fitted to carry atomic weapons.

It has been suggested that Khrushchev blundered in deciding to deploy nuclear missiles in Cuba because troops and conventional weapons alone would have prevented an American attack on the island. Kennedy would know that an encounter with Soviet troops was unthinkable because it would mean war with a superpower that possessed ICBMs capable of striking American cities from Soviet territory. A variation on that argument is that conventional weapons and the Luna missiles (which because of their short range could be used against an American army sent to invade Cuba, but could not be fired successfully against U.S. territory) would have been enough to deter an American assault on Cuba.

Why Khrushchev wanted nuclear weapons in Cuba rather than just troops, conventional weapons, and possibly the Lunas as well, can be explained by two factors. The first is that while the Soviet leader did not dismiss conventional forces as deterrents, he thought that nuclear missiles capable of striking the United States were the *ultimate* deterrent. Throughout his time as Soviet leader, Khrushchev had argued that nuclear weapons had fundamentally changed the requirements of national defense. In a speech made before a British audience in 1956, he declared:

> Everything has changed. Your specialists have told me how much they admire the battle cruiser which brought us here. Well, I'll tell you something. We will be happy to sell you this cruiser if you really want it because it's already obsolete. Its weapons have been outmoded by new weapons. Besides, cruisers like ours no longer play a decisive role. Nor do bombers. Now it's submarines that rule the sea, and missiles that rule the air.

Khrushchev's thinking on this issue was not bizarre. American leaders had themselves recently placed nuclear weapons in Britain, Turkey, and Italy in the belief that they would deter a Soviet attack on Western Europe. This was comparable to Khrushchev's installation of missiles in Cuba, the only real difference being that the Soviet leader decided to do secretly what the United States had carried out in public.

The second and more important point is that Khrushchev, as argued earlier, was not only interested in providing for the defense of Cuba. He also hoped to change the strategic balance and probably to reap other benefits, such as adding credibility to his use of nuclear brinkmanship. Troops and conventional weapons in Cuba, and even the Lunas, would not have helped to achieve those objectives.

Even though nuclear weapons better served Khrushchev's strategic aims, an argument against his decision can still be made. Soviet conventional forces in Cuba probably would have led Kennedy to forgo any plan to attack the island for fear he would engage Russian soldiers and trigger a superpower war. And a conventional military buildup in Cuba would have helped meet the Chinese charge that Moscow was failing to support revolutionary movements. In addition, Khrushchev could have altered the strategic balance and accomplished his other goals by accelerating the Soviet ICBM program and by publicizing that decision. In other words, there were other means by which Khrushchev could have achieved his policy objectives in 1962, ones that would not have moved the world to the brink of nuclear war.

In Moscow and Havana, the summer of 1962 was devoted to the refinement and implementation of Anadyr. The Ministry of Defense plan endorsed by senior Soviet officials on June 10 was honed during the following weeks and approved by Malinovsky at the time of Raúl Castro's visit to Moscow in early July. A few days later the defense minister was able to report to Khrushchev that "All the troops from the planned list of military personnel have been chosen and outfitted and are ready for transport. Plans are in place for all stages of the deployment of troops to Cuba within four months." The Soviet leader gave his final blessing to the plan that same day. On July 10 General Issa Pliyev, whom Khrushchev had selected as commander-in-chief of Soviet forces in Cuba, flew from Moscow to the Caribbean island. Everything was now in place for the implementation of Anadyr.

The dimensions of that operation were vast and the pressures involved in organizing it correspondingly great. Gribkov, a key figure in Anadyr, has recalled the stress and tension of this period. Sixteen- and eighteen-hour days meant that for Gribkov and other Anadyr planners, the summer "passed in a blur of work." The operation was readied with the speed Khrushchev requested. Beginning with the voyage of the *Maria Ulyanova* in mid-July, 85 merchant marine passenger and cargo ships, carrying men and materiel, made no less than 150 round trips between the Soviet Union and Cuba during the next three months.

The chief characteristic of Anadyr was the emphasis its overseers placed on secrecy, a concern that at times bordered on obsession. Instead of radio or telephone contact between the Ministry of Defense and the ports being used to load troops and equipment, special couriers delivered all messages.

Personnel being sent to Cuba were placed under armed guard on reaching the port of embarkation so that they could not leave the area. At the start of the voyage, the captain of the ship and the troop commander on board would not even know that Cuba was the final destination. Before departing they would receive a sealed envelope containing a smaller envelope that was to be opened once they had reached certain coordinates in the Atlantic Ocean. Only then could they read the contents of the smaller envelope to learn that their destination was Cuba. Even the name of the operation, Anadyr, was a ruse. Anadyr was a river in the northeast Soviet Union that flowed into the Bering Sea, suggesting that the operation would take place in a cold and northerly rather than a tropical location. To enhance that impression, many units sent to Cuba were provided with skis, parkas, and other winter gear.

For many of those military personnel involved in the operation, Anadyr brought extreme discomfort and a sense of disorientation. During the trip to Cuba they were allowed on deck for exercise or meals only during the night. Once a ship reached the Caribbean, even those privileges were removed. At least half of those making the trip suffered from seasickness, some chronically, and one sergeant died. His body, wrapped in tarpaulin, was cast overboard at night.

A journal kept by Colonel Arkadi Shorokhov during his crossing reveals how many of those who participated in Anadyr experienced the operation:

On 20 August we approached the Azores. There was a storm. The ship was pitching heavily. All our soldiers and officers were seasick. That night, some enterprising soldiers opened up two barrels of pickles and ate them. That eased the heaving for them somewhat. . . .

We have been sailing for weeks. All around is turquoise ocean. The heat. We strip down to our shorts. . . .

During the day, American aircraft fly over our ship. Some military vessel has been tailing our freighter and demanding inspection. We just listen over the radio, but don't reply. In the morning, the drone of an airplane wakes us. American fighter swoops down on our ship almost getting tangled in the masts. The coast of Cuba is visible now. . . .

Disembarking after so many torments, the men could be heard cursing: "You're not going to get me back on that mother ——— barge. Until they build a bridge to Russia, I'm not going over the ocean for anything."

The most curious aspect of Anadyr was the transfer of important powers to the Soviet military in Cuba. Khrushchev, although retaining tight control over use of the medium- and intermediate-range missiles, delegated to Pliyev the authority to fire the short-range, tactical Lunas in an emergency situation. The Soviet premier, who appears to have been thinking about the possibility that the Lunas might need to be used quickly if the United States suddenly invaded Cuba, did so verbally during a meeting with Pliyev in early July, in the presence of Malinovsky. This delegation of powers would later be modified, but during the summer and fall of 1962 Khrushchev made the mistake of allowing Pliyev to maintain a control over the Lunas that he should have kept for himself.

As the Soviet military buildup in Cuba began, Kennedy administration officials and their Republican adversaries took note. Their concern intensified during the autumn. Although the crisis over Cuba would not explode until mid-October, developments in the weeks preceding would shape the way the missile crisis played out.

3

An Autumn of Discontent

IN LATE SEPTEMBER 1962, Oleg Troyanovsky spoke with Khrushchev in the Soviet leader's study. After reviewing reports from his military advisers on the progress of Operation Anadyr, Khrushchev somberly declared, "Soon hell will break loose." "I hope the boat does not capsize," Troyanovsky responded. Khrushchev, deep in thought, said nothing for a moment, then reflected that it was now "too late to change anything." It seemed to Troyanovsky that the Soviet leader had at last acknowledged the magnitude of the risks involved in Anadyr—the likelihood that the United States would detect the missiles in Cuba before their deployment was complete.

These weeks immediately preceding that time in mid-October 1962 when hell did break loose were ones of frenetic activity. The Soviets pressed ahead with Operation Anadyr while offering misleading public and private assurances to the Kennedy administration that the military buildup in Cuba did not threaten American security interests. The Cubans hinted at the installation of nuclear weapons on their island. American officials, meanwhile, fashioned a public response to the deployment in Cuba, fended off Republicans who were critical of Kennedy's reaction to the buildup, intensified Operation Mongoose, and advanced the contingency plans that had al-

ready been developed for the use of force against Cuba. How
Khrushchev deceived Kennedy over the deployment in Cuba,
JFK's public commitments, and the administration's further
preparations for military action, especially during the first few
days of October, all played a role in shaping the course of the
missile crisis.

Throughout the fall of 1962, Soviet officials pressed ahead
with Operation Anadyr. The transportation of men and
conventional weaponry to the Caribbean island had been
ongoing since mid-July. When on September 8 the *Omsk*,
a large-hatch freighter, arrived in Cuba carrying the equipment needed to install medium-range missiles, the deployment of offensive nuclear weapons began. Meanwhile senior
Soviet officials continued to keep close tabs on the operation.
In early September Gribkov made a second trip to the
Crimea. Visiting Sevastopol, where three of the missile regi-
ments bound for Cuba were being loaded onto ships, Gribkov
was pleased to find that the work was proceeding with speed
and care.

In addition to monitoring Anadyr's progress, Soviet officials continued to review the details of the operation with a
view to making necessary alterations. The original plan called
for the transportation of nearly 51,000 men to Cuba. During
September, however, the decision was made to scrap some of
the naval squadrons that were to have been used, and the
number of men set to arrive in Cuba was reduced to just over
45,000. (In the end, 41,902 Soviet military personnel were on
the island when the missile crisis began.)

In reviewing Anadyr, Soviet leaders also noted the authority originally granted to Pliyev to decide whether to fire the
Lunas if the United States invaded Cuba. Khrushchev had
delegated these powers verbally to Pliyev in July, but the
arrangement had not been put in writing. On September 8 the

Ministry of Defense produced a draft for a message from Malinovsky to Pliyev, stating:

> Only in the event of a landing of the opponent's forces on the island of Cuba and if there is a concentration of enemy ships with landing forces near the coast of Cuba, in its territorial waters . . . and there is no possibility to receive directives from the U.S.S.R. Ministry of Defense, you are personally allowed as an exception to take the decision to apply the tactical nuclear Luna missiles as a means of local war for the destruction of the opponent on land and on the coast with the aim of a full crushing defeat of troops on the territory of Cuba and the defense of the Cuban Revolution.

It is not clear whether these instructions, confirming Khrushchev's delegation of authority over the Lunas, were in fact sent to Pliyev. They may have been dispatched in late September or early October. According to Gribkov, though, who claims to have brought the message to Malinovsky for final approval, the defense minister decided against transmitting it. "We don't need any extra pieces of paper," he allegedly told Gribkov. "Pliyev knows everything already." Whether or not it was sent, the drafting of the message indicates that before the missile crisis began, the authority to order the use of the Luna missiles in an emergency stayed in Pliyev's hands.

During the early fall of 1962 Khrushchev remained as convinced as he had been in the spring that Kennedy planned to attack Cuba, or at least blockade it. Developments in September strengthened that belief. Of course, the Soviet leader knew that JFK must have been concerned by the military buildup in Cuba, and that the president's interest in attacking the island may therefore have been aroused. But there were other factors too.

For one thing, Soviet diplomats confirmed Khrushchev's suspicions about the probability of an American assault on

Cuba. On September 7, for example, Ambassador Alekseyev sent a telegram to Moscow reporting on relations between Washington and Havana. Alekseyev's report was balanced: he noted that Kennedy's recent rhetoric had been less hostile than that of other American political figures, and he did not portray an American attack on Cuba as inevitable. Nevertheless there was much in Alekseyev's telegram that fed Khrushchev's anxieties about U.S. intentions. Heightened military preparations for action against Cuba, blatant acts of sabotage carried out by anti-Castro emigrés (such as the August 24 bombing of a hotel in Havana), and the hostility expressed by senators and the American press toward the present Cuban government were all reported to Moscow by Alekseyev. "One can also assume," he added, "that the most wildly aggressive powers in the USA (the Pentagon, the Cuban external counter-revolution, and others) will continue to exert pressure on Kennedy in order to realize the most decisive actions against Cuba."

Khrushchev also thought the U.S. congressional elections, now only a few weeks away in November, might encourage Kennedy to attack Cuba. JFK, the Soviet leader reasoned, might well calculate that Castro's overthrow on the eve of the election would shore up the strength of Democratic candidates and thus bolster his own political position. It was an accusation that Khrushchev would direct at Kennedy several times during the course of the missile crisis itself. But the suspicion was one he held before mid-October as well. In his September 28, 1962, message to JFK, one of several private, frank, and revealing letters the two leaders exchanged during the Kennedy-Khrushchev era, the Soviet premier suggested that Kennedy's tough stance on Cuba and other issues might be connected to the "pre-election situation in your country."

Khrushchev's anticipation of an attack on Cuba was also a

product of his confused reading of the political situation in the United States. The Soviet leader made the mistake of lumping together such different groups as the Kennedy administration, Republicans in Congress, and the press, and surmising that JFK was somehow directing or influencing all these groups. Specifically Khrushchev took the belligerence of various Republicans and members of the American press over Cuba as evidence of Kennedy's own aggressive intentions toward Castro. In discussing JFK's Cuban policies with a member of Kennedy's cabinet in early September, for example, Khrushchev talked at length about the statements being made by members of Congress.

In the fall of 1962, then, Khrushchev thought it likely that Kennedy would order an invasion of Cuba or perhaps a blockade, thereby jeopardizing the successful completion of Anadyr. To discourage JFK from taking that step, the Soviet leader tried a combination of intimidation and deceit throughout September. The intimidation consisted of threats that the Soviet Union would respond militarily if the United States invaded or blockaded Cuba. In a conversation with the Austrian vice-chancellor, Khrushchev, who must have expected the Austrians to relay his comments to officials in Washington, declared that Soviet ships would ignore any blockade, continuing en route to Cuba, and that military retaliation might well be ordered if American vessels interfered with Soviet shipping. Khrushchev also warned Kennedy in his correspondence that an American assault on Cuba would lead to "thermonuclear war."

The clear aim of these threats was to deter a U.S. attack or blockade—to convince JFK that the price, in terms of the probable Soviet response, was too high. Khrushchev also tried to persuade Kennedy that military action against Castro was unnecessary anyway by deceiving him about the nature of the buildup in Cuba. In public and private, Soviet officials insisted that the deployment involved no nuclear weapons that could be fired on the United States. Put another way, the buildup in Cuba did not represent an unacceptable threat to American security interests.

Much of this deception was practiced unwittingly by Anatoly Dobrynin, Soviet ambassador to the United States. Dobrynin, presumably at Khrushchev's request, held a number of meetings with senior officials in the Kennedy administration at the start of September. On the 4th he visited Robert Kennedy. When the attorney general explained the administration's concern over the military buildup in Cuba, Dobrynin assured him that it did not include surface-to-surface nuclear weapons. Furthermore, he said, Khrushchev would do nothing to embarrass JFK before the congressional elections. Two days later Dobrynin spoke to Theodore Sorensen. In his notes from their meeting, Sorensen wrote that Dobrynin "repeated several times . . . that they had done nothing new or extraordinary in Cuba—that the events causing all the excitement had been taking place somewhat gradually and quietly over a long period of time—and that he stood by his assurances that all these steps were defensive in nature and did not represent any threat to the security of the United States." The next day Dobrynin assured Adlai Stevenson that "only defensive weapons are being supplied" to Cuba. What made Dobrynin's explanations to American officials so convincing was the fact that Khrushchev had decided against briefing his ambassador about Anadyr. Hence when Dobrynin declared that no nuclear weapons would be installed in Cuba, he believed he was telling the truth.

In addition to using these private channels to mislead Kennedy about the military buildup in Cuba, Khrushchev also used the public domain. On September 11 TASS, the Soviet news agency, released a government statement on the situation in Cuba. In it Moscow once again declared that "The arms and military equipment sent to Cuba are intended solely for defensive purposes." As the Soviet Union already had missiles on its own territory capable of striking the United States, the statement explained, there was no need for nuclear weapons in Cuba.

Khrushchev later argued that there was no deception involved in his public and private assurances because the *objective* behind the deployment of nuclear weapons in Cuba was to deter American aggression or to defend the island if such an attack occurred. But U.S. officials were understandably concerned about the *capabilities* of the weapons being sent to Cuba, not just the alleged motivations behind their deployment. It was not surprising, therefore, that when Kennedy and his advisers learned about the presence of nuclear weapons in Cuba in mid-October, they felt Khrushchev had deliberately lied to them in September. He had. The anger of administration officials partially explains why they were so determined at the start of the missile crisis to take vigorous action to remove the nuclear weapons from Cuba.

Cuban officials, like their counterparts in Moscow, thought that American rhetoric and policies during the fall of 1962 portended an invasion of their country. In formulating an effective response to that anticipated attack, Castro and his advisers unsurprisingly placed their faith in the growing Soviet military presence on the island. As Alekseyev reported to Moscow in early September, "The Cuban leadership believes . . . that the main guarantee of the development of the Cuban Revolution under conditions of possible direct American aggression is the readiness of the Soviet government to provide military assistance to Cuba and simultaneously to warn the USA of that fact."

Of those two requirements, officials in Havana knew that Moscow was already furnishing the first—military aid, including nuclear weapons. Of the second, they understood that Khrushchev would not permit public disclosure of the missiles until deployment was complete. Thus Cuban leaders had to settle for hinting on various occasions during these weeks that nuclear weapons were being installed. On September 9, for example, Foreign Minister Raúl Roa declared during a reception at the Brazilian embassy that Soviet aid to Cuba was "in the nature of a *complete* military guarantee [my emphasis]." "If . . . we are attacked," another Cuban official told the UN General Assembly a month later, "we will defend ourselves. I repeat, we have sufficient means with which to defend ourselves; we have indeed our inevitable weapons, the weapons which we would have preferred not to acquire and which we do not wish to employ."

It is not clear whether Cuban officials made these and other remarks out of frustration with Khrushchev's secrecy, or whether they were purposely trying to deter an American attack without technically disregarding Khrushchev's wishes. Either way, the Kennedy administration failed to note the hints dropped by Havana.

The Soviet military buildup was not Kennedy's only concern over Cuba in the fall of 1962. The other was the way the Republican party was exploiting and the American press exploring this issue. Certain that attacking Kennedy's record on Cuba would help win more Republican seats in the next Congress; influenced by a sense of revenge, remembering JFK's blistering assault on Republicans during the 1960 presidential campaign for their handling of Castro; and genuinely convinced that the Soviet buildup in Cuba threatened United States security, Republicans attacked JFK mercilessly.

Kennedy was underestimating the Soviet threat in Cuba, they claimed, and he needed to respond more forthrightly.

The most common GOP argument was that Kennedy should blockade Cuba and prevent the delivery of additional Soviet troops and military equipment to the island. Some Republicans in Congress had recommended this approach before the fall of 1962. But as the Soviet military buildup in Cuba continued and the congressional elections approached, the number of Republican voices calling for a blockade increased substantially. On September 5 Senator Barry Goldwater made the case for a blockade, as, in the next few days, did South Dakota Senator Karl Mundt and Richard Nixon, who was then running for the governorship of California. Some Republicans were attracted to a more decisive application of American force. Texas Senator John Tower suggested that Kennedy extend recognition to a Cuban government in exile and then arm that group to enable them to overthrow Castro. Senator Homer Capehart, running for reelection in Indiana, went further and called for an invasion of Cuba.

Of all the Republicans who harassed Kennedy over Cuba during this period, the most vocal, influential, mysterious, and troublesome for the administration was Senator Kenneth Keating of New York. On August 31 he rose on the Senate floor to speak about Cuba, a country in which he had taken great interest since Castro came to power in 1959. The Soviets, Keating said, were sending troops to Cuba, not just technicians as JFK and his aides had reported. He described in detail the kind of military equipment that was being deployed on the island. Keating said his information came from sources whose identity he refused to reveal.

That Keating was apparently receiving reports from special informants helps explain why he became the focal point for the Republican assault on JFK over Cuba. His access to secret sources not only aroused the curiosity of the press and public, it also seemed to make his claims more credible than those of other Republicans. Keating's sources also raised the disturbing (though, in retrospect, unlikely) possibility that the Kennedy administration had been given the same information as the New York senator but had chosen to withhold it from the American people.

Keating was persistent. In an eight-week period beginning in late August, he made no less than twenty-five public statements on Cuba, some in the Senate, others on radio and television, ensuring that he and the issue remained in the spotlight. On October 10 he declared that the Soviet Union was deploying offensive, surface-to-surface nuclear weapons in Cuba— six days before Kennedy himself received intelligence data confirming this information. Keating never revealed the identity of his sources, but the most recent research indicates that his informants were from the CIA (including, perhaps, Director John McCone himself), the Defense Department, and the Cuban exile community.

Congress not only voiced its dissatisfaction with the president's Cuban policies, it also took concrete action. On September 20 the Senate passed a resolution endorsing the use of force to curb Cuban meddling in Latin America, expressing a determination to prevent the installation of nuclear missiles in Cuba, and proclaiming the need for self-determination on the island—and, by implication, the removal of Castro. Six days later the House voted in overwhelming support of that resolution, and also approved a bill cutting off aid to nations that permitted their merchant ships to transport weapons or other commodities to Cuba. In early October, Congress voted to terminate economic and military aid to any country that "sells, furnishes, or permits any ships under its registry" to trade with Castro's Cuba, a decision that provoked a storm of

protest from Britain and Sweden. Although Democrats generally made support for these initiatives bipartisan, it was
clearly the Republicans who were setting the congressional
agenda on Cuba.

The press added to the pressure mounting on the Kennedy
administration. All recent presidents have been very concerned about the way they are portrayed in the media, knowing this can affect their political credibility and their
popularity with the American people. But none more so than
Kennedy. The attention JFK devoted to this issue throughout
his presidency set a pattern for his successors. So when most
newspapers expressed their support for Republican proposals
on Cuba, JFK took note.

In the fall of 1962, then, two factors—the Soviet military
buildup on the island and domestic political reaction—were
forcing Kennedy to consider action over Cuba. Of the two, it
appears that Kennedy was more concerned with the second, in
part because he assumed the Soviet deployment in Cuba did
not include nuclear weapons. A third factor, more subtle, was
Operation Mongoose's momentum that existed irrespective of
what the Soviets were doing in Cuba or what Republicans
were saying.

In defining his position on Cuba during these weeks,
Kennedy's thinking was clearly influenced by the information
he received about the Soviet buildup on the island. Although
John McCone had predicted the Soviets would place nuclear
weapons in Cuba, the majority view in the intelligence community and in the State and Defense departments was that
they would not do so because this would be inconsistent with
Soviet practice: Moscow had never before installed nuclear
weapons outside the Soviet Union. This assumption proved
false and contributed to the misinterpretation of intelligence
data. Not until mid-October did the CIA uncover the pres-

ence of missiles in Cuba; until that time Kennedy examined
the question of the Soviet military buildup in the Caribbean
assuming that no nuclear weapons were being installed.

Surprisingly, a number of American officials thought Soviet military aid was intended to deter or defend against an
American attack on Cuba, rather than a deliberate provoca-
tion to the United States. In a special national intelligence esti-
mate prepared in September, CIA officials concluded that
"the main purpose of the present military buildup in Cuba is
to strengthen the Communist regime there against what the
Cubans and Soviets conceive to be a danger that the US may
attempt by one means or another to overthrow it." A military
aide informed Vice-President Lyndon Johnson at the start of
October that "the primary aim of Soviet policy in Cuba is to
prevent a liquidation of the Castro regime." A few pundits
were making the same observation publicly. Veteran journalist Walter Lippmann wrote on October 9, "It is obvious . . .
that Castro is being armed against a re-run of the raid on the
Bay of Pigs." When the missiles were discovered, American
officials virtually to a man looked on Khrushchev's actions in
Cuba as unjustifiably provocative, assuming that nuclear
weapons, unlike conventional forces, were not needed for the
defense of Cuba.

In crafting his policies toward Cuba in the fall of 1962,
Kennedy, as he had done earlier, developed a two-track approach. He used the public domain to pursue his objectives
while at the same time promoting a covert solution to the
Cuban problem. Before August 1962 JFK's public policies
were consistent with his private actions: both sought to remove Castro from power. In the two months before the missile crisis, however, public and private goals diverged. At the
covert level the president and his advisers accelerated Operation Mongoose and the contingency planning for military ac-

tion against Cuba. But in public Kennedy underplayed the significance of developments in Cuba, arguing that the Soviet military buildup there did not threaten vital American interests because it did not include nuclear weapons.

A number of factors prompted the president to adopt this public position. The Soviets had assured him privately that no offensive missiles would be sent to Cuba, as in Dobrynin's conversation with Robert Kennedy. Hence JFK felt he could say the buildup was not a threat. Perhaps more important, he wished to speak out on Cuba in order to defuse the public concern that Republicans had generated over his reaction to the buildup on the island. On September 4 Senator Keating appeared on NBC television, once again criticizing the Kennedy administration over Cuba. An angry Pierre Salinger, press secretary to the president, immediately called network officials to complain about the inaccuracies in Keating's statements. He promised that Kennedy would "deal with those inaccuracies" later that same day.

In seeking to rebut Republican criticisms, such as those made by Keating, the president must have been aware of their impact not only on his administration's credibility but on the prospects of Democratic candidates in the congressional elections. A formal statement read out by Pierre Salinger on September 4 acknowledged that Khrushchev had recently sent anti-aircraft missiles, radar, motor torpedo boats, and military technicians to Cuba. All that, however, did not threaten American security because there was "no evidence of any organized combat force in Cuba from any Soviet bloc country; of military bases provided to Russia; of a violation of the 1934 treaty relating to Guantanamo; of the presence of offensive ground-to-ground missiles; or of other significant offensive capability either in Cuban hands or under Soviet direction and guidance. Were it to be otherwise, the gravest issues would arise."

Nine days later Kennedy spoke in person to the press, making a preliminary statement and then fielding questions. Once again, he claimed the buildup was merely defensive, as weapons that could be fired on the United States were not being sent to Cuba. He went on to make explicit the commitment that was implicit in this assertion, namely that nuclear missiles in Cuba would threaten American security and so force the Kennedy administration to act. That pledge proved to be of considerable importance to the course of the missile crisis. Knowing that he had promised the American people he would respond vigorously to an offensive missile deployment in Cuba, Kennedy felt he had no alternative at the start of the crisis but to take decisive action. Throughout the confrontation he remained committed to securing the removal of the nuclear weapons in part because of the public pledges he had made in September.

While Kennedy's covert policies were generally far less moderate than his public pronouncements on the Cuban situation, he was nonetheless restrained in his approach to the question of the Jupiter missiles in Turkey. This issue became increasingly linked to the Cuban situation because nuclear weapons on the Soviet border could be viewed as an American analogue to the Soviet buildup in Cuba, especially when the aid being sent by Moscow was found to include missiles.

The origins of the Jupiters-in-Turkey policy lay in the Eisenhower years. The idea of supplying nuclear weapons to American allies was first put into practice when the Eisenhower administration pledged sixty Thor missiles to Britain to help repair the damage done to the "special relationship" between the United States and Britain by the 1956 Suez crisis. Soviet technological breakthroughs, particularly the successful 1957 launch of Sputnik, furthered Eisenhower's interest in deploying intermediate-range ballistic missiles in Europe to shore up the defense of the West. Only Turkey and Italy, however, were willing to accept the nuclear weapons offered. In October 1959 it was agreed that Washington would furnish Turkey with fifteen Jupiters, with the Turks owning the missiles and the United States retaining control of the warheads. Any decision to fire these weapons would require the approval of both the American and Turkish governments.

Contrary to what many participants in the missile crisis and those who have studied it assumed, the Eisenhower administration did not in fact deploy the Jupiters in Turkey. Construction of the missile sites had not even started when Kennedy became president. He therefore had the opportunity to revoke the agreement with the Turks if he so desired. Shortly after his inauguration, the Joint Congressional Committee on Atomic Energy provided the White House with a report recommending the cancellation of the Jupiter deployment in Turkey. The Jupiters were already becoming obsolete, the committee pointed out. Because they burned liquid fuel, the Jupiters required several hours of preparation before they could be fired. They would be exposed and immobile, vulnerable to a Soviet first strike. It would be better, the committee advised, to replace the Jupiters with missile-firing Polaris submarines in the Mediterranean. A report on NATO (North Atlantic Treaty Organization) filed by Dean Acheson in March 1961 also advocated cancellation of the plan to put Jupiters in Turkey.

Kennedy appears to have been influenced by this advice. At the end of March he asked a special group, consisting of officials from State, Defense, and CIA, to "review the question of deployment of IRBM's to Turkey and make recommendations to him." A month later Rusk asked Turkish Foreign Minister Selim Sarper whether his government would agree to scrap the plan to deploy the Jupiters. Sarper balked at the proposal, saying it was "necessary [to] go through with [the] project for political and psychological reasons." By June 1961 Kennedy's advisers were equally reluctant to discard the Jupiter plan. In the aftermath of the Vienna summit, at which Khrushchev had been so aggressive, and with a new crisis brewing over Berlin, the Soviets might interpret a cancellation of the missile deployment in Turkey as a sign of weakness. So Kennedy proceeded with the deployment. It appears that the Jupiters were sent to Turkey in the fall of 1961 and became operational in the spring of 1962.

Kennedy, however, remained skeptical about the value of the Jupiters, and in the spring of 1962 his advisers started to reexamine the question. Rusk again put the idea of removing the missiles to the Turks at a May 1962 NATO meeting, but he found them to be as committed to the Jupiters as they had been a year earlier. On Kennedy's instructions, George Ball and Defense Department official Paul Nitze raised the issue with the Turkish ambassador to the United States later in the summer—again, to no avail.

The effect of the Soviet military buildup in Cuba was to strengthen Kennedy's interest in withdrawing the Jupiters from Turkey. In National Security Action Memorandum No. 181, issued on August 23, 1962, McGeorge Bundy wrote:

> The President has directed that the following actions and studies be undertaken in the light of new Soviet bloc activity in Cuba.
>
> 1. What action can be taken to get Jupiter missiles out of Turkey? (Action: Department of Defense). . . .

Since at this point Kennedy anticipated that the Soviet deployment in Cuba would not include nuclear missiles, he was
probably thinking that the removal of the missiles from
Turkey would make it more difficult for the Soviets to justify
the buildup of military personnel and conventional weapons
in Cuba. It appears that the Defense Department took no action before the start of the missile crisis to bring about the
withdrawal of the Jupiters.

In later years Robert Kennedy and others claimed that the
president had ordered the removal of the Jupiters from
Turkey before the missile crisis began, and that he was sur-
prised to learn in the midst of the confrontation that his decision had not been carried out. This argument does not hold
water. As Barton Bernstein and Philip Nash, the two leading
authorities on the Jupiter issue, have written, Kennedy wished
to remove the missiles from Turkey and instructed his subor-
dinates to find out whether the Turks would agree to that
course of action, but at no point before the October 1962 crisis
over Cuba did he *order* their withdrawal from Turkey.

In retrospect, it may well have been a good thing that the
president did not order the removal of the Jupiters. Their
presence in Turkey was probably not a major factor in Khrushchev's decision to deploy missiles in Cuba, and they provided the superpowers with an additional and perhaps
essential mechanism for defusing the crisis. In the end, the Soviet leader promised to withdraw the missiles from Cuba in
return for a public commitment from Kennedy not to invade
the island and a private promise to remove the Jupiters from
Turkey. Khrushchev may have felt that a no-invasion pledge
by itself was not a sufficient inducement to remove the nuclear
weapons from Cuba. But that guarantee along with the pledge
to withdraw the Jupiters were enough for the Soviet premier.

Despite his prudence in handling the Jupiter issue,

Kennedy displayed less caution in the rest of his covert policies. In the fall of 1962 he intensified Operation Mongoose, accelerated the development of contingency plans for military
action against Cuba, and allowed further military maneuvers
in the Caribbean. Historians remained largely ignorant of
these aspects of JFK's Cuban policies until quite recently, and
the new findings have raised the startling question of whether
Kennedy would have ordered an attack on the island even if
missiles had not been deployed there.

By mid-summer 1962 the first stage of Operation Mongoose, focused on intelligence collection, drew to a close. Lansdale, in an administration debate over the goals of Mongoose,
urged other American officials to be more ambitious. In early
August, for example, he asked the Defense Department and
the Joint Chiefs of Staff to prepare a report outlining the
"Consequences of (US) Military Intervention (in Cuba) to include cost (personnel, units and equipment), effect on world-
wide ability to react, possibility of a requirement for sustained
occupation, the level of national mobilization required, and
Cuban counteraction." The gap between Lansdale's expectations and the reality of an undesirable Cuban government not
only retaining power but now bolstered by Soviet military aid
created a frustration that caused some in the administration to
entertain extreme possibilities. At an August 10 meeting one
official, apparently Secretary of Defense McNamara, called
for the assassination of Castro and other prominent Cuban officials.

On August 23 Kennedy brought this debate to an end by is-
suing National Security Action Memorandum No. 181, a policy directive that defined the second phase of Mongoose. In
"Operation Mongoose Plan B Plus," American officials were
authorized to encourage an internal uprising against Castro
that could be used to justify U.S. military intervention. In

other words, the restrictions imposed on Mongoose in the early part of 1962 were to be lifted. Kennedy also called for intensified contingency planning for military action against Cuba.

The new directives in NSAM-181 were soon put into effect. CIA officials monitored internal conditions in Cuba, evaluating prospects for an anti-Castro uprising. In several reports in late August and early September, the idea of an imminent insurgency was seriously entertained. "Apparently by mutual consent among the large counter-revolutionary groups," one report stated, "the date for the uprising has been delayed by about two weeks, and is now scheduled for 15 September or thereafter."

When his aide Arthur Schlesinger fired off a memorandum to Kennedy expressing concern over CIA interest in an anti-Castro revolt and raising the possibility of whether anyone "down the line is encouraging the Cubans into rash action," the president responded by saying he knew nothing of the uprisings that had been predicted. He asked Schlesinger to send him the relevant intelligence reports and promised to take the matter up with the CIA. Even if Kennedy had not in fact seen the CIA reports on the prospects for a revolt, Schlesinger's intervention would have ensured that he acquired them. In other words, the president must have been aware that his own intelligence people were talking about the likelihood of an uprising in Cuba. At the very least, the CIA reports would have prompted discussion within the administration of aid to the anti-Castro rebels, especially since Operation Mongoose, as Kennedy had defined it on August 23, now encompassed that policy option.

The planning needed either to offer military aid to the rebels or to take direct military action against Cuba regardless of its internal situation was developed during September with great urgency. OPLAN 312, the air-strike option, was honed. On September 18 the air force carried out training exercises in which planes embarked on missions approximating those they would fly in an assault on Cuba. Ten days later Admiral Dennison approved the blueprints produced by the air force for an attack on Cuba. Kennedy, it should be noted, took an active interest in the formulation of these plans.

In the early days of October administration officials considered whether to take this planning a step further. McNamara, in particular, called for heightened preparations for military action against Cuba with great zeal. Admiral George Anderson, who was in charge of naval operations during the missile crisis, recalled in 1987 that both he and the newly appointed chairman of the Joint Chiefs of Staff, General Maxwell Taylor, felt at the time that McNamara was readying American military power because he thought Mongoose might trigger an anti-Castro uprising on the island—which Kennedy could then use in justifying a decision to attack Cuba. "I think he was prepared to exploit any developments that took place," Anderson said of McNamara.

After an October 1 meeting between McNamara and the JCS, directives were issued for the attainment of "maximum readiness" to carry out an air strike or invasion by October 20. As later clarified, this was not a date set for the start of hostilities but the point at which preparations for military action were to be complete. On the evening of October 1 Admiral Dennison ordered fleet commanders "to take all feasible measures necessary to assure maximum readiness to execute CINCLANT OPLAN 312 [the air strike option] by October 20." The same day army commanders were informed that the invasion plan might soon be put into effect. In line with a deci-

sion taken at the October 1 meeting, Dennison began on October 3 to take the preliminary steps needed for the establishment of a blockade around Cuba.

These military preparations involved far more than just the
fine-tuning of contingency plans on paper; they demanded the
actual movement of forces and equipment. Ammunition and
supplies were positioned at Florida bases; a squadron of fighters and aviation equipment were stationed at the Key West
base; and a naval vessel was sent south from Norfolk, Virginia. Vice-Admiral William Mack, one of those involved in
this planning, recalls that the administration was "moving
troops and moving aircraft from Bragg and Hawaii. Actually,
getting ready to invade Cuba is what we were doing." All
these military steps taken before October 16 proved to be important in that they influenced the thinking of American officials once the missile crisis occurred. To a degree, they gave
Kennedy and some of his advisers the sense that a military reaction to the missiles in Cuba was a good idea because the
United States was already in a position to respond in that way.

To conceal these military preparations, a practice amphibi-
ous assault on the Caribbean island of Vieques off Puerto Rico
would be staged on October 15. Similar to maneuvers held
earlier in the year, this one was aimed in part at intimidating
Havana. The Pentagon told journalists that the mission was to
liberate Vieques from a fictional dictator called Ortsac. Few
could have failed to notice that spelled backward the name
read Castro.

The scope of these preparations for military action against
Cuba would seem to validate Khrushchev's fear, which in part
lay behind his decision to place nuclear weapons on the island,
that Kennedy would attack Cuba unless deterred by Soviet
power. But it could also be said that this American activity in
early October was only a reflection of Washington's concern

over the Soviet military buildup in Cuba. In other words, without Operation Anadyr these preparations for military action against Cuba would not have taken place. Perhaps, but the development of contingency plans for Cuba was well under way before the military buildup on the island had begun; the internal momentum of the planning process might have culminated in the early October decisions for enhanced preparations regardless of Soviet actions in Cuba.

The intensification of Operation Mongoose paralleled the heightened military preparations and intersected with them. Pentagon officials continued to think that a Mongoose-provoked, anti-Castro uprising in Cuba might be needed before their plans could be implemented. By early October, however, a feeling pervaded the CIA and Defense Department that support for Operation Mongoose was waning. Robert Kennedy disabused CIA and Defense officials of that notion in no uncertain terms during an October 4 meeting of the Special Group (Augmented). He reported the president's irritation at the operation's lack of success, especially with sabotage. When McCone stated that "hesitancy" among administration officials had hindered Mongoose's progress, Bobby Kennedy "took sharp exception stating the Special Group had not withheld approval on any specified actions to his knowledge, but to the contrary had urged and insisted upon action by the Lansdale operating organization."

After a frank discussion, it was agreed that "more dynamic action" was needed. Lansdale was instructed to carry out immediately all acts of sabotage that had been scheduled and to plan for new ones; to present a scheme for mining Cuban harbors; and to examine the feasibility of seizing Castro supporters for interrogation. The restrictions first imposed by Mongoose's overseers, already lessened in August, were now reduced even further.

Lansdale wasted no time putting Mongoose's operational representatives to work on these recommendations. By October 11 he was able to offer three concrete proposals in line with the call for more dynamic approaches: using time-delay fuses to destroy Cuban-owned ships, especially those docked at Cuban or Soviet bloc ports; transmitting Voice of America radio broadcasts in Russian in order to undermine the loyalty of Soviet technicians on the island; and developing a capability to drop balloons over Cuba containing anti-Castro and anti-Soviet propaganda. As Lansdale described this last plan, "Helium-inflated balloons will be launched at night from a foreign flag ship in international waters at least ten miles off the coast of Cuba." A Cuban emigré would charter the ship and would avoid using U.S. ports, tactics obviously intended to mask CIA involvement. By October 15 the State Department had approved Lansdale's three proposals.

The next day, Tuesday, October 16, Mongoose planners met in Robert Kennedy's office to discuss the operation's progress. As in the October 4 session, the attorney general emphasized the "general dissatisfaction of the President" with Mongoose. The operation had been in existence for a year, he observed, and though improvements had been made in the collection of intelligence, nothing had been done to influence Cuba's internal political situation. Pledging to give the operation more of his personal attention, he announced that he would now meet every morning with Mongoose's operational representatives. Toward the end of the meeting, Robert Kennedy spoke of "the change in atmosphere in the United States Government during the last twenty-four hours." That deliberately vague statement was a reference to the fact that earlier in the day the president and his leading advisers had learned that there were nuclear weapons in Cuba. The missile crisis had begun.

4

Week One: How to Respond

BEING PRESIDENT, John Kennedy often observed, would be "the best job in the world if it weren't for the Russians. . . . You never know what those bastards are up to." He could never have been more convinced of this assertion than on October 16 when he learned that Khrushchev had done what he and almost all his advisers were certain he never would: place missiles in Cuba, a mere ninety miles off the coast of Florida.

Photographs taken by a U-2 plane during an October 14 flight over Cuba revealed nuclear weapons on the island. The CIA gave the information to McGeorge Bundy, who in turn passed the news to JFK on the morning of October 16. Kennedy, still in bed, was livid. Khrushchev "can't do this to me," was the sense of his initial response, recalled Bundy. Robert Kennedy, always protective of the president, was even more enraged. His reaction, after examining the photographic evidence of the missile sites, was one of utter dismay: "Oh shit! Shit! Shit! Those sons of bitches Russians."

The realization that the Soviets had lied about the military buildup in Cuba provoked the Kennedys' fury. Time and again that fall, both publicly and in private, Soviet officials had informed their American counterparts that the weapons being sent to Cuba were for purely defensive purposes. "It had all been lies," Robert Kennedy later reflected. "One gigantic fabric of lies. We had been deceived by Khrushchev, but we had also fooled ourselves."

The anger of the Kennedys also related to their fears about the political damage this revelation might cause. On September 4 and 13 JFK had declared that he would not tolerate nuclear weapons on the island. Once he and his advisers were briefed on October 16 about developments in Cuba, they felt the president's public commitments ruled out the possibility of simply accepting the missile deployment. Not only would that inaction erode America's credibility overseas, with allies as well as enemies, it would, perhaps more disconcertingly, damage the administration's image before the American people. JFK's earlier declarations on the Soviet buildup in Cuba were certainly on his mind when he learned of the missiles, for he immediately asked a close adviser to check his public statements on U.S. reaction to a deployment of missiles in Cuba.

To help him craft a response to Khrushchev's missile gambit, and to assist him generally in managing the crisis that would no doubt unfold, Kennedy decided on a series of meetings with his senior advisers. This group of officials later became known as the executive committee of the National Security Council, or ExComm for short. Two ExComm meetings were held on the opening day of the missile crisis, the first convening in the cabinet room shortly before midday. Unbeknownst to the other officials present, Kennedy had arranged for these meetings to be taped, with microphones concealed in the drapes, thus bequeathing to historians a record of the proceedings. As the president was aware that his words were being recorded for posterity, the performative aspect of his participation in ExComm should be considered. Still, it is reasonable to assume that his statements in these meetings reflected his true feelings.

In the first ExComm session, on Tuesday, October 16, Kennedy discussed the extent to which news about the missiles in Cuba should be circulated, even within his administration. He decided to keep the information a closely guarded secret. Officials would be briefed only on a need-to-know basis. "We've got to keep it as tight as possible," Kennedy explained, "particularly what we're going to do about it. Maybe a lot of people know about what's there, but what we're going to do about it really ought to be . . . the tightest of all because otherwise we bitch it up." The president knew that if the news leaked, Khrushchev might accelerate the installation of missiles in Cuba or take other action that would limit U.S. options.

But the focus of concern in the first ExComm meeting was how to respond to the Soviet missile deployment. Kennedy's views on this issue were clear. He presented a case that he would make several times during the day, namely that the United States had no choice but to respond with force, and that the only real question was the sort of military action to be carried out. He listed the options: "One is the strike just on . . . these three bases. . . . The second is the broader one . . . which is on the airfields and on the SAM [surface-to-air missile] sites and on anything else connected with . . . [the] missiles. Third is doing both of those things and also at the same time launching a blockade." Robert Kennedy added another choice: invading Cuba. Enumerating the options later in the discussion, JFK settled on three: an air strike limited to the missile sites; a more general strike, not only on the missile sites but on other military installations as well; and an invasion.

After lunch Kennedy spoke privately with Adlai Stevenson, again indicating his preference for a military response. "We'll have to do something quickly. I suppose the alternatives are to go in by air and wipe them out, or to take other steps to render the weapons inoperable." Stevenson, troubled by JFK's belligerence, recommended that an effort be made to achieve a peaceful solution before resorting to an air strike.

Kennedy left the White House in late afternoon and motored to the State Department auditorium where he spoke off the record to five hundred newspaper editors and broadcasters. Although he wished to keep the crisis over Cuba secret, the subject was clearly uppermost in his mind as he ruminated on the dangers of the Soviet-American rivalry and the responsibilities of leadership in the nuclear age. "I don't think it is unfair to say that the United States—and the world—is now passing through one of its most critical periods," Kennedy observed. Reciting a bullfighter's poem, which spoke to the differences between his relationship and that of his audience to the challenges of the cold war, he said:

> Bullfight critics ranked in rows
> Crowd the enormous Plaza full;
> But only one is there who knows.
> And he's the man who fights the bull.

The ExComm group reconvened in the early evening. Kennedy, as in the first meeting, continued to favor a military response in Cuba. He argued that the limited and general air strikes, along with the invasion, were the only feasible U.S. alternatives. Of the three, he seemed to favor the general air strike. Other options, such as the establishment of a naval blockade around Cuba or the use of a more diplomatically centered strategy (perhaps trading the Jupiters in Turkey for the missiles in Cuba), had no appeal for the president at this point.

What is difficult to establish is why Kennedy supported military action at the start of the missile crisis. Certainly it was not because he thought the missiles in Cuba radically altered the strategic balance between the superpowers; he did not, pointing out that ICBMs on Soviet territory could already reach the United States. Nor was it because he believed Khrushchev intended to fire the nuclear weapons in Cuba at the United States. "You assume," he stated, while probably thinking of his country's capacity to launch a retaliatory nuclear strike, "they wouldn't do that."

The anger Kennedy felt over Khrushchev's deceit, with his promises of only a defensive buildup in Cuba, partly explains the president's initial leanings toward military action. His awareness of the public commitments he had made in September—he did mention them in ExComm that day—to take decisive action if missiles were put in Cuba also influenced his thinking. Of all the options, initiating military action was clearly the most decisive.

Another factor of likely importance was American military planning and the actual movement of men and materiel that had taken place before October 16. To Kennedy, military action may well have seemed a good idea because the United States was already in a position to carry it out. JFK and his advisers devoted some time to this issue in ExComm. In the first session the president asked, "How long did it take to get in a position where we can invade Cuba? Almost a month? Two months?" The discussion in the second ExComm meeting again covered the subject of precrisis preparations for an attack on Cuba, with McNamara assuring his colleagues that "the military planning has been carried on for a considerable period of time, is well under way. And I believe that all the preparations that we could take without the risk of preparations causing discussion and knowledge of this, either among our public or in Cuba, have been taken and are authorized."

JFK was not alone among American officials in calling for military action. Lyndon Johnson, Maxwell Taylor, and Secretary of the Treasury Douglas Dillon all agreed with the president on this. Robert Kennedy also leaned toward a military approach, apparently preferring an invasion. When during one of the October 16 ExComm meetings he passed his famous note to JFK—"I now know how Tojo felt when he was planning [the Japanese attack on] Pearl Harbor"—the comment seems to have been meant literally.

Other officials explored the alternatives to air strikes. Most important, McNamara introduced the idea of establishing a naval blockade around Cuba; and by the end of the second ExComm session this seemed to be his preference. Rusk wondered whether a diplomatic approach might not be adopted. A warning letter could be dispatched to Castro, he argued, and the services of the OAS could be enlisted to increase pressure on the Cuban leader. Under Secretary of State George Ball, as he would do more famously in later years in the debate over fighting a land war in Vietnam, spoke passionately against the use of force. "This come in there on Pearl Harbor just frightens the hell out of me as to what's going beyond," he declared.

In retrospect it is fortunate that JFK did not feel obliged to make a quick decision on October 16. If he had, the weight of evidence indicates he would have ordered military action, probably a general air strike. That would surely have provoked a Soviet response, from Cuba or at another point on the globe or both, which may well have produced the nightmare everyone had been hoping to avoid since 1945: a war between the world's two superpowers, both armed to the teeth with nuclear weapons.

WEDNESDAY, OCTOBER 17

By Wednesday morning Kennedy had not changed his outlook. In a meeting with two senior aides he once again spoke in favor of an air strike. He explained that the recent congressional resolution on Cuba provided him with the authority he needed to take military action; and so, as one adviser present noted, he "seemed inclined to act."

Deciding to keep to his planned schedule in order to avoid arousing press suspicion, Kennedy hit the campaign trail in Connecticut where he spoke on behalf of Democrats running for office there in the November elections. Before his departure for New Haven, the president instructed John McCone to visit Dwight Eisenhower at his farm in Gettysburg, Pennsylvania.

Interested in generating bipartisan support for his administration's handling of the crisis in Cuba, as well as picking the brains of a former president with vast experience in military affairs, JFK must have been pleased to learn that Eisenhower's views mirrored his own. After receiving a briefing from McCone, Eisenhower professed to be unsurprised by Khrushchev's gamble. The former president argued that verbal complaints to the Soviets would have no effect. Nor was a blockade likely to work. Even if a Soviet ship laden with military equipment was stopped, Eisenhower pointed out, there would still be the problem for the United States of what to do with that vessel. Rather than supporting diplomacy or a naval quarantine, Eisenhower, as McCone recorded in his notes from the meeting, "seemed to lean toward (but did not specifically recommend) military action which would cut off Havana and therefore take over the heart of the government. He thought this might be done by airborne divisions." "Revisionist" historians of Eisenhower like to portray him as a man of moderation in comparison with a president such as Kennedy. It is interesting to note that in their initial reactions to the news of the missiles in Cuba, Eisenhower and Kennedy showed few differences.

Given JFK's absence on Wednesday from his administration's ongoing discussion of the Cuban situation, the ExComm meetings that day were unrestrained. Officials felt no need to tailor their views to match the president's. In these sessions some officials appeared to vacillate between the available options, unable or unwilling to commit themselves. Ball, although commenting again on the dangers of military action, including the possibility that it would "throw the NATO allies in disarray," discussed a number of alternatives that included a limited air strike.

Despite individual uncertainties, the views of most ExComm officials began to coalesce around two options: a blockade (or quarantine) and an air strike. Blockade supporters included Llewellyn Thompson, former U.S. ambassador to the Soviet Union, and State Department official Edwin Martin. Among those who favored the air strike were John McCone and Maxwell Taylor.

In this debate the two officials who expressed their views with the greatest passion were Robert Kennedy and Dean Acheson, the former secretary of state who was one of JFK's informal advisers. The interest that the attorney general had shown the previous day in an invasion of Cuba now evaporated. Picking up on the "Pearl Harbor" comparison that Ball

had first made, Robert Kennedy based his arguments on ethi-
cal considerations. A military strike would betray American
values, kill thousands of innocent Cuban civilians, and destroy
the moral authority of the United States government at home
and around the globe. The president, who would become
known as the Tojo of the 1960s, would be personally damaged
if he authorized such an attack.

Dean Acheson, the intimidating embodiment of the American Establishment, replied strongly. The United States
had told Moscow that a missile deployment in Cuba was
unacceptable, Acheson pointed out, whereas the Japanese had
issued no comparable warning before the attack on Pearl
Harbor. Hence the analogy with 1941 was preposterous. The
key issue was one of time. If a blockade were established, the
Soviets would be able to make the missiles in Cuba operational and so would be in a position to retaliate from there
should the United States later decide on military action. An
air strike on the missile sites, executed immediately and
without warning, was the better approach. Unlike the blockade, it would actually remove the nuclear weapons; and it was
a low-risk strategy because, with the Soviet missiles not yet
operational, Khrushchev could not order a nuclear response
from Cuba. Acheson made it clear that he favored a surgical
strike on the missile sites. He did not wish to attack other Soviet military installations in Cuba, as did several of the other
hawks.

In addition to the blockade and military action, a third
option began to emerge on October 17: the use of diplomacy
to secure the withdrawal of the missiles from Cuba. Charles
Bohlen, Kennedy's newly appointed ambassador to France,
and Adlai Stevenson were the two officials who proposed
this alternative course. In that day's ExComm meetings,

which he attended before leaving for Europe, Bohlen made the case that negotiations should be tried first. He argued

> against any action against Cuba, particularly an air strike without warning, stating such would be divisive with all Allies and subject us to criticism throughout the world. He advocated writing both Khrushchev and Castro; if their response was negative or unsatisfactory then we should plan action; advise our principal allies, seek a two-thirds vote from the OAS and then act.

Throughout the rest of the discussion, Bohlen stuck to his guns despite a lack of support for his proposals. In a way, this October 17 discussion was a forerunner to the ExComm meeting on October 20 when Stevenson, alone, argued that negotiations with the Soviets needed to accompany the establishment of a blockade around Cuba.

Stevenson's October 17 memorandum to the president reflected his initial feelings and warned of the dangers of rash military action. "To start or risk starting a nuclear war is bound to be divisive at best," Stevenson observed, "and the judgments of history seldom coincide with the tempers of the moment." Specifically he recommended that Moscow and Havana be told that the missiles must be withdrawn, otherwise the United States would be compelled to take military action. But to increase the likelihood that Khrushchev and Castro would bite the bullet, Kennedy should make clear that he was prepared to discuss the withdrawal of the Jupiters from Turkey and Italy. Kennedy was not only unpersuaded by Stevenson's proposals, he was annoyed by them.

As American officials secretly debated strategy on Wednesday, their counterparts in Moscow were enjoying the successful launch of Cosmos 10, the first Soviet reconnaissance satellite. After a mere four days it was pulled out of orbit, suggesting that Soviet officials were anxious to interpret the photographic evidence it had collected. The intelligence data gathered by Cosmos 10 may have included information about the military buildup in the southeastern United States that the Joint Chiefs had accelerated on October 17.

THURSDAY, OCTOBER 18

By Thursday morning President Kennedy still believed that a general air strike on Cuba was his best option. When his advisers talked about the merits of the blockade in that morning's ExComm meeting, he was skeptical. That approach, he observed, would not remove the missiles already in Cuba and would prompt Khrushchev to seize Berlin. "The blockade wouldn't be sufficient," Kennedy maintained. He went on to explain, assessing the various military alternatives, why he thought the general strike would be more effective than an invasion. With the latter, thousands of Americans would be killed in Cuba, and "That'd be much more of a mess than you are [in] if you take out these [missiles with a strike]." An air strike had the advantage of being quick and decisive, unlike an invasion that would inevitably be drawn out. A strike would present Khrushchev with a *fait accompli* in the same way that the Soviets' crushing of the 1956 Hungarian uprising had left President Eisenhower no option but to accept that unsavory episode.

Robert Kennedy, by contrast, remained attached to the blockade, though he paid lip service to the air strike in this ExComm meeting, especially after his brother had indicated his preference for it. Although the commonly held view is that Robert Kennedy valiantly led the blockade supporters against the hawks throughout the first week of the missile crisis, it was Llewellyn Thompson who spoke most authoritatively, clearly, and extensively on behalf of the quarantine during the October 18 ExComm session. McNamara, not Robert Kennedy, led the discussion when the president left the meeting. Of course Robert Kennedy's views were most important in the sense that the president was more likely to be swayed by him than by anyone else. Nevertheless it is fair to say that the leadership among ExComm's blockade supporters was provided alternately by Thompson, McNamara, and Robert Kennedy.

The course of the ExComm discussion on October 18 was revealing in other ways. For instance, it indicated the extent to which the president and his advisers were aware, even at this early stage in the crisis, of the relevance of the missiles in Turkey and, to a lesser degree, those in Italy. Robert Kennedy pointed out that the Soviets could say there was no difference between nuclear weapons in Cuba and those in Turkey, while President Kennedy, Thompson, and McNamara suggested that the removal of the Jupiters was a possibility.

The October 18 ExComm discussion also showed that many American officials viewed the removal of Castro, and not just the nuclear weapons in Cuba, as an optimal objective. Thompson argued that the pressure generated by a blockade around Cuba could lead to Castro's downfall. Robert Kennedy, considering the drawbacks of a quarantine, wondered whether a blockade had "ever brought anybody down," thereby implying an interest in overthrowing the Cuban leader. Toward the end of the discussion, one official, who seemed to note these comments, recalled that "we were hoping last night we'd get the collapse of Castro?" "Well, you might get [it]," interjected another Kennedy adviser. All this shows the influence on the ExComm debate of pre-missile-crisis thinking, particularly the preparations for military action against Cuba. The immediate objective of removing the missiles from Cuba did not, in many cases, deflect American officials from their earlier goal of ousting Castro.

This ExComm meeting also touched upon the issue of the upcoming congressional elections. Kennedy critics have sometimes wondered whether his administration's determination to confront Khrushchev over the missiles in Cuba was created or at least strengthened by a desire to reap the electoral benefits of a foreign policy success. Evidence supporting that theory has been scant. Douglas Dillon's note to Sorensen on October 18, asking whether consideration had been given to "the very real possibility that if we allow Cuba to complete installation and operational readiness of missile bases, the next House of Representatives is likely to have a Republican majority," is the only clear sign that a Kennedy adviser's views were affected by an awareness of the elections. And this was rather bizarre because Dillon was himself a Republican. There are, however, two references by Robert Kennedy to the November elections at the October 18 ExComm meeting, although the precise wording of his comments cannot be determined because of the poor quality of recently released tape. Even this means that the sum of the evidence available to support the idea that the congressional elections were an important influence on the administration's thinking *during* the missile crisis remains unimpressive.

Although the ExComm meeting on Thursday morning encompassed a wide range of issues, it evolved into a simple binary debate over the merits of the blockade and air strike alternatives. For the supporters of military action, men such as McCone, Taylor, and Acheson, the key issues continued to be the ineffectiveness of the blockade and the readiness of the missiles. They believed that a quarantine, while preventing the Soviets from sending more nuclear weapons to Cuba, would not help remove the missiles already on the island. A direct military assault could achieve that objective. This sort of military action needed to be carried out quickly, however, before the missiles were ready to be fired on the United States. Although Taylor on October 18 called for an invasion of Cuba, most of the hawks wanted a quick air strike.

For the blockade supporters, their main concerns were the likelihood that Khrushchev's response would be more severe if Kennedy authorized military action than if he established a quarantine, and the inflexibility of the military options compared with the blockade. Unlike an air strike or invasion, blockading Cuba would not preclude other alternatives— such as negotiations or the later use of force.

Just before he left the ExComm meeting early Thursday afternoon, the president urged his advisers to bring the debate on the blockade and air strike to a close, requesting a "final judgment on all these questions." From the course of the discussion so far, it was clear that the diplomatic approach championed by Bohlen and Stevenson had, for all intents and purposes, been rejected by their colleagues.

Outside the ExComm group, the advice JFK sought on Thursday mirrored the divisions within ExComm. Acheson, given the opportunity to put his case to the president in private, insisted that the Pearl Harbor analogy was false and that the air strike was the best option. But Robert Lovett, a former secretary of defense much respected by the president, argued that a blockade was the safer bet. It was less likely than an air strike or invasion to produce a Soviet military response.

Taking time out from these intense, secret discussions on the Cuban situation, Kennedy kept an appointment with Gromyko, a meeting that had been scheduled before the start of the crisis. Reading from a prepared text, the Soviet foreign minister stressed Moscow's concern over the "unabated anti-

Cuban campaign in the United States, a campaign which was apparently backed by the United States Government." He argued that Kennedy's policies were a threat to Cuban independence, and warned that the Soviet Union, as "a great and strong nation, . . . could not stand by as a mere observer when aggression was planned [against Cuba]." Hence Khrushchev's decision to supply military aid to Castro, which, Gromyko insisted, was "solely for the purpose of contributing to the defense capabilities of Cuba" and furthering its economic development.

Responding to Gromyko's lengthy statement, Kennedy was anxious to avoid revealing that he knew of the missiles in Cuba. That would keep the initiative in Washington. So although Kennedy thought about embarrassing Gromyko by showing him pictures of the missile sites that were in the top drawer of his Oval Office desk, he resisted the temptation. "Our presumption was that the armaments supplied by [the] USSR were defensive," JFK told Gromyko, and he planned neither to invade nor blockade Cuba. Despite keeping his cards close to his chest, Kennedy pointed out that the Soviet military buildup in Cuba had produced "the most dangerous situation since the end of the war"—a comment Gromyko might have interpreted as indicating American awareness of the missiles but apparently did not.

From the time he received the news of Khrushchev's missile placement until Thursday morning, Kennedy had believed that a general air strike would be the most effective American response. During the course of October 18, however, his views changed dramatically. He first showed signs of shifting ground in his afternoon meeting with Acheson, when he used the Pearl Harbor analogy to highlight the concern he felt about attacking Cuba. A discussion with ExComm officials in the evening strengthened the president's interest in a blockade. By then, the balance of opinion within the group was shifting toward the quarantine, a consensus Kennedy said he found satisfying.

In withdrawing his support for the air strike, the president appeared to be swayed by the arguments of the blockade proponents—that with a quarantine it was *less* likely that Khrushchev would respond militarily by, for instance, seizing Berlin; the United States would not be viewed as an international pariah for carrying out a surprise, Pearl Harbor–style attack; and other options—air strike, invasion, and diplomacy—would still be available.

An additional factor was the Bay of Pigs disaster. Kennedy knew from the events in April 1961 that his military and intelligence officers, who were among the leading hawks during the missile crisis, were capable of gross errors of judgment. In October 1962 he did not, as he had before April 1961, assume their virtual infallibility on military matters. Relying on his own abilities and those of his civilian advisers, especially Robert Kennedy, he felt more comfortable rejecting their recommendations than he had at the start of his presidency. In this way the lessons of the Bay of Pigs helped Kennedy evaluate the advice he received during the first week of the October crisis with a critical eye.

By the evening of October 18, then, Kennedy's preference had switched to the quarantine. Discussions over the next three days converted that provisional decision into a clear commitment to blockade Cuba.

FRIDAY, OCTOBER 19, TO SUNDAY, OCTOBER 21

Still anxious to avoid arousing the suspicion of the press, Kennedy set out on Friday to campaign in Ohio and Illinois, as scheduled. Before leaving, he met with his senior advisers, telling Robert Kennedy to fashion a consensus in ExComm in favor of the blockade. If that could not be achieved, the president observed, "I'll make my own decision anyway."

During the ExComm meeting that day, American officials failed to develop the sort of consensus the president wanted. McGeorge Bundy opened the discussion on options by making it clear he favored an air strike. In a classic explanation of the hawk position, he said he doubted

> whether the strategy group was serving the President as well as it might, if it merely recommended a blockade. He had spoken with the President this morning, and he felt there was further work to be done. A blockade would not remove the missiles. Its effects were uncertain and in any event would be slow to be felt. Something more would be needed to get the missiles out of Cuba. This would be made more difficult by the prior publicity of the blockade and the consequent pressures from the United Nations for a negotiated settlement. An air strike would be quick and would take out the bases in a clean surgical operation. He favored decisive action with its advantages of surprise and confronting the world with a fait accompli.

In turn, Acheson, Dillon, McCone, and Taylor expressed their agreement with Bundy's recommendations.

McNamara, however, did not. Although assuring the hawks that the necessary military preparations would be taken to ready the air force for a strike, he said he preferred a blockade. Robert Kennedy now entered the fray to great effect. Stressing again the moral dimension, he argued that the air strike was unacceptable given "the memory of Pearl Harbor and with all the implications this would have for us in whatever world there would be afterward. For 175 years we had not been that kind of country. A sneak attack was not in our traditions. Thousands of Cubans would be killed without warning, and a lot of Russians too." A blockade would "make known unmistakably the seriousness of United States determination to get the missiles out" while at the same time giving the Soviets "some room for maneuver to pull back from their over-extended position in Cuba."

Despite the provisional decision that the president had seemed to make the night before in favor of a blockade, Friday's ExComm debate appeared to be heading for a cul-de-sac. To move the discussion along, Rusk proposed the division of ExComm into two groups. One, headed by Deputy Under Secretary of State for Political Affairs Alexis Johnson, would consist of the blockade supporters; the other Bundy-led group would comprise the hawks. Both were charged with producing a draft explaining in detail their policy preference. Rusk's proposal in effect strengthened the hand of the blockade supporters, for when the two groups merged again they had succeeded in producing a far more comprehensive and compelling draft than the hawks. No less than two hours were spent evaluating the Johnson scenario; only thirty minutes were devoted to the Bundy draft. Toward the end of the meeting, Robert Kennedy again indicated his strong support for the blockade, declaring that "it was now pretty clear what the decision should be."

Cutting his trip short, President Kennedy returned to Washington from Chicago on the morning of Saturday, October 20. He met his ExComm advisers within an hour of his arrival at the White House, but not before being briefed by his brother about the debate that had taken place during his absence. In the ExComm session that afternoon, the president sought a collective confirmation of the decision in favor of the blockade that he had provisionally made on Thursday evening. Revealing the extent to which he had been influenced by Robert Kennedy's moralistic arguments, the president asked his advisers to focus their attention on the implementation of the blockade, which he saw as the only approach consistent with American principles. The air strike that some officials had recommended would run the unacceptable risk of very high American, Soviet, and Cuban casualties.

Although Kennedy now expected his advisers to fall in line behind the blockade, Stevenson had other ideas. Drawing on his reserves of courage—for he knew his views were not shared by others and that the president did not particularly value his counsel anyway—Stevenson argued that a quarantine, though preferable to a military strike, was not by itself an adequate response to the situation in Cuba. At the same time he announced the blockade, Kennedy should unveil a diplomatic package aimed at defusing the crisis quickly. In return for the removal of the missiles from Cuba, the United States should agree to withdraw the Jupiters from Turkey and Italy, abandon the navy's Guantánamo base in Cuba, and promise not to invade the island.

Shocked by a proposal that seemed to them hideously reminiscent of 1930s-style appeasement, several ExComm officials sharply condemned Stevenson's plan of action. The president objected too. Giving up Guantánamo, he said, would make America look weak, and although withdrawing the missiles from Turkey and Italy might ultimately be necessary, that issue should not be explored unless the Soviets raised it. Stevenson argued that only compromise would settle the crisis, so American concessions would have to be made. Kennedy remained unpersuaded.

For his performance that Saturday afternoon, Stevenson was attacked by his ExComm colleagues in the press once the crisis was over. It is interesting to note, however, that in the end Kennedy did promise not to invade the island and did agree privately to remove the Jupiters (though Stevenson as-

sumed this would be public knowledge). To be sure, by bringing Guantánamo into the equation Stevenson exaggerated the
scope of the concessions needed to compel Khrushchev to
back down. But the assumption on which his arguments were
built, that the missile crisis would be resolved only through
mutual concessions, was sound enough. And his desire to
achieve a quick settlement before an accident or a gradual escalation of tensions converted the crisis into war was sensible.
Stevenson was a thoughtful and sophisticated thinker. How
the confrontation over Cuba would have played out had
Kennedy implemented Stevenson's proposals (or a version of
them) is one of the most interesting "what if" questions con-
cerning the missile crisis.

Stevenson's role also highlights one of ExComm's weaknesses as a policy deliberating body: its lack of ideological
breadth. Other liberal Democrats who may well have shared
the ambassador's interest in a quick diplomatic settlement,
such as Richard Goodwin, Chester Bowles, and Arthur
Schlesinger, were excluded from the group. This ensured that
Stevenson was isolated and that the alternative course he
mapped out would not receive the attention it merited.
Kennedy's advisers and historians have often praised Ex-
Comm for generating an unrestricted debate over options. But
the way the president decided the composition of the group
meant that subtle but important ideological parameters were
in place during ExComm's discussions. They prevented the
debate from being as wide-ranging as it could and probably
should have been.

Ironically Stevenson may have strengthened Kennedy's
hand in his effort to cement a pro-blockade consensus within
ExComm. The hawks, of course, wanted an air strike. But
given a choice between the blockade and a blockade coupled
with a diplomatic deal involving significant American conces-

sions, the former option must have seemed more acceptable than it had before. Regardless of the advisers who refused to jump on the blockade bandwagon, Kennedy resolved on Saturday to blockade Cuba, a decision he would confirm after consulting with air force officials the next day.

Against the background of these ongoing secret discussions in ExComm, preparations continued for a military confrontation in the Caribbean. On Saturday morning McNamara ordered four tactical squadrons to be ready to carry out an air strike on Cuba, in the event the president decided at the last moment to implement that course of action. Meanwhile southern Florida and the Guantánamo base were reinforced, and four destroyers were stationed between Cuba and the Florida coast.

On Sunday, October 21, Kennedy met with a group of officials that included General Walter Sweeney, commander-in-chief of the Tactical Air Command. During the discussion Sweeney admitted it was unlikely an air strike would destroy all the missiles in Cuba that had been detected by American intelligence, even if everything went perfectly. Soviet nuclear retaliation from Cuba was therefore a possibility, not only if the island were blockaded but with an air strike too. For Kennedy, that realization was the clincher. He made the final decision to blockade Cuba, a course of action he would explain to the American people and the international community in a radio and television address the next day.

Sorensen, the speechwriter who composed so many of the famous phrases now associated with the Kennedy years, continued to work on an address that he had begun writing Friday. By Sunday the text was nearing completion as Sorensen produced his fourth draft. Keeping the crisis over Cuba a secret right up to the moment when Kennedy delivered that speech required hard work on Sunday. Despite the administration's best efforts, news of the missiles in Cuba and the impending crisis was about to break in several major newspapers. Kennedy himself called Max Frankel of the *New York Times* and Philip Graham at the *Washington Post*, urging them to hold their stories. McNamara made the same request to John Hay Whitney, publisher of the *New York Herald Tribune*. Convinced of the seriousness of the situation, all three agreed to cooperate.

While the ExComm group secretly weighed its options during these days, Soviet and Cuban officials tried to determine whether their American counterparts had discovered the missiles and were thus planning to attack the island. Those in Washington and Havana had very different views of these issues. Soviet diplomats in Washington did not suspect that JFK knew about the nuclear weapons in Cuba, and felt certain he was not about to order military action. On October 18, for example, Ambassador Dobrynin dispatched a telegram to Moscow explaining that the Kennedy administration was more interested in isolating Cuba from other Latin American countries and weakening its economic ties with the Soviet bloc than in attacking or blockading the island. According to the ambassador, fear of a Soviet response, probably in Berlin, accounted for JFK's reluctance to use force against Cuba. Dobrynin concluded that Cuba was "not the main issue for the USA. The West Berlin issue at present remains sharpest and most fraught with dangers."

The next day Gromyko sent a telegram from Washington to Moscow echoing Dobrynin's sentiments. Like the ambassador, he believed Kennedy intended to focus on "obstructing Cuba's economic relations with the USSR and other countries," hoping this would create the widespread dissatisfaction needed to trigger an anti-Castro uprising. Soviet assistance to

Cuba, the foreign minister argued, had deterred Kennedy from attacking the island. In addition, recently published public opinion polls showed that most Americans were against that sort of operation, and Congress (which had been pressing for a more aggressive approach toward Cuba) had gone into recess. "A USA military adventure," Gromyko confidently concluded, "is almost impossible to imagine." Of course, the foreign minister's analysis was based on the assumption that Kennedy did not know of the missiles in Cuba, a belief that had been strengthened by the president's comments during their meeting the day before.

Officials in Cuba were reading the situation rather differently. Malinovsky had sent General Gribkov and other Defense Ministry officials to Cuba to oversee the final stages of Operation Anadyr. Arriving on October 18, Gribkov met the following day with Pliyev, the man in charge of Soviet forces in Cuba. After reiterating Pliyev's earlier orders—that he must not launch the MRBMs or IRBMs without express permission from Moscow but could fire the Lunas in an emergency—Gribkov learned from Pliyev of the American U-2 reconnaissance flights that had been taking place with increasing regularity since October 14. It was therefore possible that American intelligence had discovered the nuclear weapons. Adding to Gribkov's irritation, Pliyev admitted that work at the missile sites was behind schedule. This report, Gribkov recalled, was "like a cold shower."

Gribkov then visited Raúl Castro. "Anatoli," the Cuban defense minister stated, "we have received a very important communication. On 14 October, an American U-2 reconnaissance plane photographed the area of San Cristobal where your missile sites are being built." On hearing confirmation of Pliyev's report, Gribkov ordered a greater effort to conceal the missile sites and to strengthen the guard around them in case the United States attempted sabotage. He followed this with personal inspection tours of Soviet missile sites and fighting units on October 20 and 21.

At the end of each day Gribkov reported his findings to Malinovsky by encoded telegram to Moscow. Presumably he told the defense minister about the U-2 flights, making clear that this meant the Americans probably knew about the missiles in Cuba. This reflected poorly on the implementation of Anadyr, which was Malinovsky's responsibility, so the defense minister may not have hurried to transmit this news to Khrushchev. Nevertheless Gribkov's findings suggest that senior Soviet officials may have been alerted to the possibility of Kennedy being aware of the nuclear weapons in Cuba even before October 22.

MONDAY, OCTOBER 22

Kennedy and his advisers spent Monday preparing for the public presentation of both the information they had received about the Soviet buildup in Cuba and the response they had formulated to it. The president's television and radio address, set for 7 p.m., would seek to win the support of Americans at home and influence people overseas. Attempts would also be made to enlist the support of Congress, the United Nations, the Organization of American States, and partners in the Western alliance. Strong backing from these quarters, officials in Washington calculated, would give their chosen strategy of a naval blockade a sense of legitimacy and would increase their chances of success in the confrontation over Cuba that lay ahead.

Kennedy met with his advisers in the morning. As in the October 18 ExComm session, they showed a clear interest in using the Jupiters in Turkey and Italy as a way of settling the crisis. Two different but related proposals emerged from these discussions. One was to call for UN inspection teams to be sent to the missile sites in Cuba, Turkey, and Italy, as a way of ensuring that these weapons were not fired. Another was a straight swap: removal of the missiles in Turkey and Italy in return for the withdrawal of those in Cuba. The position JFK came to adopt was that the UN observation idea should be explored in the first instance, but that this was to be viewed as an intermediary step toward the reciprocal removal of the nuclear weapons. Evidence suggests that by October 25 the president had begun to take action on the Jupiters along these lines.

Another aspect of the Jupiter issue that Kennedy considered at this meeting was the danger of his commanders in Turkey firing their missiles without first seeking presidential approval. Like Khrushchev later that day, Kennedy moved to make the crisis safer by insisting that his military officers consult him before being allowed to launch the missiles. "We don't want them firing them without our knowing about them," he told his advisers. McNamara, it emerged during the course of the discussion, had already cowritten orders to that effect. The Joint Chiefs had insisted that such instructions were already in place, hence the orders were superfluous. Some of Kennedy's aides agreed. "I'm sure we indoctrinated them not to fire any first weapons," one official argued, "they really are indoctrinated." Despite such assurances, Kennedy decided that fresh orders would be issued to hammer home the point that presidential permission was required before the Jupiters could be fired. The caution JFK showed on this issue was a sign of the prudence he would generally display during the second week of the missile crisis.

When ExComm reconvened in the afternoon, Kennedy showed signs of shifting ground on the Jupiters. Previously he had dwelled on the parallels between the missiles in Cuba and the Jupiters, hence the potential of the latter to help settle the crisis. Just a few hours before his television address, however, the president's immediate concern was how best to explain the American case to the public. From that perspective, the analogue between the missiles in Cuba and those in Turkey and Italy looked less a blessing. Critics might well argue that the blockade was an overreaction, as Moscow had been forced to live with the Jupiters in Turkey.

In "selling" the blockade to the public, therefore, it was in Kennedy's interests to argue that a comparison between the missiles in Cuba and the Jupiters was unsound. Accordingly he spoke to his advisers at the 3 p.m. meeting about "the question of distinguishing between Soviet missiles in Cuba and United States missiles in Turkey and Italy." He proposed that "everyone be fully briefed as to why these situations with respect to the deployment of missiles do not match." Unlike the installation of American missiles in Europe, he observed, the Soviets had put nuclear weapons in Cuba secretly. Kennedy's need to refute the Cuba–Turkey/Italy analogy did not mean that he had abandoned the idea of a trade involving the Jupiters; but it probably did reduce his interest in making this sort of deal in the first day or two after his television address.

Following this ExComm session, Kennedy briefed his cabinet and then a delegation from Congress on the situation in Cuba. The president wanted bipartisan support for the blockade, but he found the leadership on Capitol Hill in a less than cooperative mood. Senator Richard Russell of Georgia, in particular, vented his feelings. "Seems to me that we're at a crossroads," he told Kennedy. "We're either a first class power or we're not." The quarantine was inadequate, Russell argued. A military attack was needed to destroy the missiles in Cuba.

William Fulbright echoed Russell's criticisms. The president stuck to his guns, defending the blockade with vigor.

Throughout Monday, preparations were made to ensure that Kennedy's address was well received by allies and the international community in general. Dean Acheson met with General Charles de Gaulle in Paris; other American officials briefed British Prime Minister Harold Macmillan, West German Chancellor Konrad Adenauer, and Canadian Prime Minister John Diefenbaker. Although Macmillan thought the blockade would be difficult to enforce, and de Gaulle wondered how it could lead to the removal of the missiles already in Cuba, all the allied leaders, apart from Diefenbaker, provided Kennedy with unwavering support during the crisis.

The administration, meanwhile, began to activate the UN and OAS. Adlai Stevenson informed UN Secretary General U Thant of Kennedy's speech and of the administration's intention to convene a special meeting of the Security Council. At the same time Latin American leaders were given the text to the president's speech, either in full or summary, a letter from Kennedy, and a copy of the resolution that the United States was about to submit to the OAS.

As these steps were being taken, Rusk invited Dobrynin to his State Department office. He gave the Soviet ambassador the text of Kennedy's address as well as a private letter from the president to Khrushchev. Dobrynin responded by condemning JFK's actions as provocative and inquiring as to why Kennedy had not raised these issues during his conversation with Gromyko on October 18. He also promised that the Soviet Union would meet these threats with stiff resistance.

After his meeting with congressional leaders, Kennedy returned to his quarters to change clothes for his 7 p.m. television address. Bemused by his stormy meeting with congressional leaders, he told Theodore Sorensen: "If they want this job, they can have it—it's no great joy to me." He entered the Oval Office at 6:55. Around 7 p.m. his secretary Evelyn Lincoln moved toward him to brush his hair. As she did so, a television announcer came on the air, and Kennedy waved her away. Then he began to speak.

5

Week Two: How to Defuse

JOHN KENNEDY REVEALED to a stunned television and radio audience on Monday evening, October 22, that "offensive missile sites" were being built in Cuba. That Soviet action threatened the Western Hemisphere, he argued, violated the UN Charter, and ignored the recent congressional resolution and his own public warnings on September 4 and 13. In making the case that missiles in Cuba were intolerable, JFK stressed the issue of deception. Both the Soviet government in its September 11 statement and Gromyko in his meeting with Kennedy on October 18 had declared that no offensive weapons would be sent to Cuba, assurances that were entirely misleading. While the United States itself had dispatched missiles to other countries in the past, those initiatives had always been preceded by public warnings.

After reflecting on how the 1930s had demonstrated the importance of confronting rather than appeasing aggression, Kennedy went on to list the steps his administration would take to meet the Soviet threat in Cuba. He would blockade the island, heighten surveillance of the military buildup there, reinforce the Guantánamo base, and call meetings of the OAS and UN. A missile attack launched from Cuba against any country in the Western Hemisphere, Kennedy also declared, would compel him to order a nuclear strike on the Soviet Union.

Kennedy completed his list of initiatives by calling on Khrushchev "to halt and eliminate this clandestine, reckless and provocative threat to world peace and to stable relations between our two nations. I call upon him further to abandon this course of world domination, and to join in an historic effort to end the perilous arms race and transform the history of man." It is interesting to note that in his early drafts Sorensen had included a far more specific proposal in place of this rather general plea. "I am asking Soviet Chairman Khrushchev, who will shortly be coming to the United Nations meetings in New York," Sorensen had written, "to meet with me at the earliest opportunity with respect to this provocative threat to world peace and to the relations between our two countries." As he was revising the speech, however, Sorensen received a memorandum from the president's Republican aide Douglas Dillon, advising him to eliminate the section calling for a New York summit meeting. "It sounds very weak compared to [the] other items," Dillon argued, "and gives [the] impression of a lot of talk and no action which is an impression the President must avoid above all others."

Dillon's memorandum to Sorensen was in a sense a reflection of the general feeling in the administration, evident in the rejection of Stevenson's recommendations in ExComm on October 20, that Kennedy's initial response to the missile deployment in Cuba should not include specific proposals for negotiation. (Dillon was among those who had attacked Stevenson at the ExComm session.) In any event, Sorensen took Dillon's advice and, presumably in consultation with the president, removed the reference to a Khrushchev-Kennedy summit.

After completing his list of policy initiatives, JFK moved on to a part of the speech that has often been overlooked by historians. "I want to say a few words to the captive people of Cuba," he stated, "to whom this speech is being directly carried by special radio facilities." Kennedy declared that Castro had betrayed the 1959 revolution by turning Cuba into a Soviet base. Noting that the Cuban people in the past had often risen up to cast out dictators, he expressed his belief that "most Cubans today look forward to the time when they will be truly free." This was an obvious attempt to encourage the Cuban people to work for Castro's overthrow. The objective that several American officials had defined in ExComm during the first week of the missile crisis, namely the need to secure the removal of both the nuclear weapons *and* the Cuban leader, was evidently still an administration goal.

One other noteworthy aspect of the speech was Kennedy's prediction that "Many months of sacrifice and self-discipline lie ahead—months in which both our patience and our will will be tested—months in which many threats and denunciations will keep us aware of our dangers." Kennedy anticipated a long, drawn-out struggle, not, as would turn out to be the case, a settlement of the crisis within six days.

Although the president did not finally decide to blockade Cuba until October 21, Sorensen had begun to produce a draft of JFK's speech two days earlier—in other words, at a point when Kennedy's choice of the quarantine option was not yet certain. For this reason Sorensen produced another version of Kennedy's address, one he would make if he decided to carry out an air strike on Cuba. That draft has a chilling quality with apocalyptic overtones. To be delivered shortly after the attack had taken place, Kennedy would begin the speech by saying:

My fellow Americans:

With a very heavy heart, and in necessary fulfillment of my oath of office, I have ordered—and the United States Air Force has now carried out—military operations, with conventional weapons only, to remove a major nuclear weapons build-up from the soil of Cuba. This action has been taken under Article 51 of the United Nations and in fulfillment of the requirements of national safety. Further military action has been authorized to ensure that this threat is fully removed and not restored.

"The tragedy here—self-evidently—is in the loss of innocent lives on all sides," Kennedy would go on to say. "For the United States I hereby accept responsibility for this action and pledge that all appropriate efforts will be made, on request, to assist the families of these innocent victims."

After learning that Kennedy was about to make a speech of great importance, Khrushchev hastily convened a meeting of senior officials in the Kremlin in what was the middle of the night in Moscow. Analyzing the text of JFK's address together, their initial reaction, as one Soviet official recalls, was one of "relief rather than anxiety." A blockade left "a lot of room for political maneuvering, the more so because the President called the blockade a 'quarantine' which created an illusion of still greater vagueness.... It did not look like an ultimatum or a direct threat of attacking Cuba." At the same time there is no record on this occasion of any discussion among the Soviet leaders of backing down by removing the missiles from Cuba. Accordingly Khrushchev began fashioning an indignant response.

Just as Kennedy had made the crisis less dangerous on October 22 by reminding his military commanders that they could not fire Jupiters from Turkey without his approval, so

Khrushchev that same day took similar steps with the Luna missiles in Cuba. A telegram dispatched to Havana late at night ordered Pliyev to ready Soviet forces for a military engagement, but it also canceled the arrangement permitting Pliyev to fire tactical nuclear weapons in an emergency without Khrushchev's permission. This limitation was spelled out by Moscow again later in the crisis. It reduced the likelihood that an American attack on Cuba would lead to nuclear war.

In line with Moscow's instructions and those issued by Castro, Soviet and Cuban forces on the island prepared for battle with all possible speed. "General Pliyev's senior staff," one Soviet official recalls, "spent a sleepless night in hurried but calm work to boost the readiness of the Soviet Group of Forces." Meanwhile Castro ordered a nationwide mobilization. No less than 270,000 Cubans, according to one well-informed source, were armed and ready to fight within a few days of Kennedy's speech. The Cuban general staff had devised a plan of action whereby the island would be divided into western, central, and eastern zones, each with its own military command, in the event of an American attack. If the U.S. invasion force managed to prevail in one area of the island, Cuban forces would still be able to fight independently in the other sectors. Castro would take charge of the western zone, Major Juan Almeida the central, and Raúl Castro the eastern. While the American military anticipated a quick and decisive victory, their Cuban counterparts were confident that any engagement would prove far more protracted.

As Kennedy's October 22 speech brought news of the crisis over Cuba to Americans and other peoples, many were gripped by fear, even terror. After hearing the president's address, a young girl in Portland, Oregon, went to her bedroom to pray. A father of three in Illinois charted a course for fresh water in Canada. Housewives emptied supermarkets across the United States. "They're nuts," said one grocer. "One lady's working four shopping carts at once. Another lady bought twelve packages of detergents. What's she going to do, wash up after the bomb?" Americans were not the only ones preparing for the worst. In Havana a young mother covered herself and her son with olive oil, believing it would help repel napalm.

With nuclear war a real possibility, millions of people suddenly acquired a heightened sense of their own mortality. Latin Americans knew that Soviet missiles in Cuba could strike many of their cities. Europeans were aware that a Soviet-American conflict in the Caribbean could spread to their continent via Berlin or perhaps Turkey. American, Cuban, and Soviet citizens, in particular, lived during these days with the prospect of nuclear annihilation. An October 23 Gallup poll revealed that one of five Americans thought the naval blockade around Cuba would bring about World War III.

TUESDAY, OCTOBER 23

On Tuesday Khrushchev sent to Kennedy the letter he had begun to draft the previous night. A sense of indignation permeated his message. "I must say frankly that the measures indicated in your statement constitute a serious threat to peace and to the security of nations." The blockade was illegal, the Soviet premier claimed, and the weapons being sent to the Caribbean were only for Cuba's defense—in other words, there was no sinister ulterior motive. Khrushchev concluded by calling on Kennedy to cancel the blockade.

The unwavering determination that Khrushchev had demonstrated in his message to Kennedy was also apparent in the steps taken that day by the Soviet Union and its allies in preparation for a military showdown. The combat readiness of Soviet and indeed all Warsaw Pact forces was heightened. The planned demobilization of older contingents of troops and of the Soviet submarine fleet was postponed.

Throughout the crisis Khrushchev and his advisers relied on Dobrynin, their ambassador in Washington, for updates on the situation. They particularly sought his insights on the Kennedy administration's thinking and possible next move. In his October 23 telegram, Dobrynin reported that the Kennedy team was not ready to back down over Cuba. McNamara, he explained, had briefed journalists that the United States would sink missile-carrying Soviet ships if they tried to penetrate the blockade. The next day Khrushchev decided against challenging the quarantine. Dobrynin's report may have influenced his thinking on this matter.

As for his policy recommendations, Dobrynin played the role of both hawk and dove. On the one hand, he maintained that it was necessary to "demonstrate the resolve of the USSR" and that blockading the ground routes to West Berlin might be the best way to do so. On the other hand, he argued that this sort of action should be put on hold for a while, as "an extreme aggravation of the situation, it goes without saying, would not be in our interests."

At the two ExComm meetings held that Tuesday, Kennedy and his advisers prepared for the quarantine and fine-tuned their contingency plans for military action. The president approved the wording of the proclamation that would formally initiate the blockade. Difficulties in enforcing the quarantine were discussed, and procedures for dealing with uncompliant Soviet vessels were established. The U.S. navy would fire at the rudders and propellers of any such ship in order to stop it without provoking a major engagement. It was agreed that vessels clearly carrying military equipment would be intercepted, though merchant ships might be allowed to pass.

Although Kennedy was placing his faith in a blockade at this point, he was anxious that preparations for a military attack on Cuba be advanced so that this option would be available to him at a moment's notice: "The only thing I say once again is that if the Russians' response makes a military action or invasion inevitable, I want to be able to feel that we will not have to waste any days having to get ready." Led by McNamara, ExComm officials discussed the logistics of an invasion of Cuba. Approximately 130 merchant ships, the secretary of defense explained, would be needed, and the Defense Department had begun chartering some of them the previous day.

ExComm officials recognized that an attack on Cuba might lead to a Soviet retaliatory strike on the American mainland, so they considered both the military and civilian implications of that nightmare scenario. Kennedy authorized a photographic mission over airfields in Florida to make sure U.S. planes were not positioned wingtip to wingtip, thereby making them an easy target for a Soviet attack. When it was discovered that they were indeed positioned that way, the president ordered their dispersal. The ability of the civilian population to withstand a missile strike from Cuba was also discussed. Pentagon officials explained that while the 1,100-mile-range Soviet MRBMs in Cuba could hit an area populated by 92 million Americans, unequipped fallout shelters were available for only 40 million. Kennedy ordered the formulation of a civil defense plan for the southeastern part of the country that could be implemented during an invasion of Cuba.

After the second ExComm session on Tuesday had finished, JFK talked in his office with aide Kenneth O'Donnell,

Ted Sorensen, and Robert Kennedy. The president, who had recently read Barbara Tuchman's book *The Guns of August*, reflected on the miscalculations of the great powers that had led to war in 1914—and in 1939. With these troubling precedents in mind, he expressed his determination to make sure that 1962 would not mark the start of World War III. "We were not going to misjudge . . . or precipitously push our adversaries into a course of action that was not intended or anticipated," was the thrust of his remarks, Robert Kennedy recalled. Generally speaking, JFK's leadership during the second week of the missile crisis was characterized by this sort of caution and skill—qualities that had often been lacking in his handling of the Cuban situation before October 1962.

Kennedy replied to Khrushchev's message in the early evening. While he accused the Soviet Union of provoking the crisis and warned that Russian ships must not challenge the blockade, his letter also displayed a more moderate tone. "I am concerned that we both show prudence," he wrote, "and do nothing to allow events to make the situation more difficult to control than it already is." The president also signed Proclamation 3504 in a White House ceremony that evening, thereby formally establishing the blockade that was to take effect the next day.

A great effort was made on October 23 to galvanize support for the American position from international organizations, Capitol Hill, and the media. Rusk put the administration's case to the OAS, winning unanimous backing for a resolution that called for the immediate withdrawal of the missiles from Cuba. Stevenson presented a vigorous defense of American policy in the UN Security Council. McCone spoke to congressional leaders, who were more supportive than they had been the day before, and to a group of distinguished journalists.

Kennedy, meanwhile, courted Henry Luce, president of Time, Inc., inviting him to the White House for a special briefing.

Focusing on the establishment of the blockade, preparations for a possible attack on Cuba, and the presentation of their case to the public, Kennedy and his advisers devoted relatively little time to the key question of what to do should the quarantine fail to effect a withdrawal of the missiles from Cuba. Two matters that did concentrate the minds of the Kennedy team were Berlin and the overthrow of Castro. Worried about Soviet reprisals in Europe, the president asked the CIA to analyze the impact of a Soviet blockade on West Berlin, and established a special ExComm subcommittee on the German city. Kennedy's concern about Berlin was perhaps unwarranted. Although Dobrynin had talked that very day about blockading Berlin, Khrushchev was not of a like mind. When Deputy Foreign Minister Vasily Kuznetsov proposed upping the ante in Berlin, Khrushchev treated the idea with contempt. An aide present during the conversation concluded that the Soviet leader had no interest in expanding the geographic boundaries of the crisis. Like Kennedy, Khrushchev demonstrated more caution and common sense during the missile crisis than he had before it.

Some U.S. officials continued to regard the removal of Castro, in addition to the nuclear weapons, as the best possible outcome. In his meeting with the congressional leadership, John McCone stated that "our purposes must be to remove the missiles and also to remove Castro." For those officials who shared it, this sentiment represented a real weakness in their approach to the Cuban crisis. It skewed their thinking, distracting them from what was clearly the only matter of immediate concern: removing the missiles from Cuba without getting into war. It made their attitude toward negotiations with the Soviets less flexible in the sense that they would rather not approve a settlement that included an American promise not to attack Cuba at some later date. This aspect of the administration's thinking would have mattered little had it not been for the fact that Kennedy, as his comments later in the week made clear, was one of those who wished to retain the use of force against Cuba as a policy option after the crisis.

In the early evening of October 23, Kennedy asked his brother to pay Dobrynin a visit in order to explain to him the seriousness of the situation. Angry and agitated in his meeting with the Soviet ambassador, Robert Kennedy launched into a searing attack on recent Soviet policy. He reviewed developments during the early fall—how Moscow had promised the Kennedy administration that no offensive missiles would be placed in Cuba; how those assurances had prompted the president to tell the American people that the situation was not critical; and how the detection of missiles in Cuba showed that Soviet officials had lied. The result of all this, Robert Kennedy lamented, was that his brother "felt himself deceived, and deceived intentionally. He is convinced of that even now. It was for him a great disappointment," and that feeling had colored his speech the previous evening.

Dobrynin responded by asking the question that some Western critics would later pose: Why had the president chosen a public confrontation over Cuba instead of private diplomacy? JFK could have conveyed his concerns to Gromyko in their October 18 meeting or used other "confidential channels." Being frank with Gromyko, Robert Kennedy responded, would have been pointless given the hostile tone the foreign minister had adopted in his talk with the president, and his unwillingness even to acknowledge the existence of nuclear weapons in Cuba. When asked directly whether his superiors in Moscow had confirmed to him that there were offensive missiles on the island, Dobrynin fell into Robert Kennedy's neatly laid trap. There had been, the ambassador said, no reason for him to believe that claim. "There, you see," the attorney general chipped in, "what would have been the point of us contacting you via the confidential channel, if, as it appears, even the Ambassador . . . does not know that long-range missiles which can strike the USA . . . have already been provided to Cuba[?]"

During the rest of the meeting Dobrynin stressed Khrushchev's desire to maintain good relations with President Kennedy. Robert, who appeared to the ambassador to have calmed down by this point, said his brother felt the same way about his personal relationship with Khrushchev. Moving toward the door, he asked whether his brother's speech and the blockade proclamation had altered the instructions given to the captains of Soviet vessels heading toward the quarantine line. Dobrynin explained that he had not been advised about this, but he did know that Soviet ships had been ordered a month earlier to ignore any blockade imposed by the United States. "I don't know how all this will end," Robert Kennedy reflected as he waved goodbye to Dobrynin, "for we intend to stop your ships."

By the late evening, no end to the missile crisis was in sight. Neither Moscow nor Washington had advanced a diplomatic settlement. War, potentially nuclear war, seemed a real possibility. The indiscreet comments of some added to that sickening feeling. Mikhail Polonik, Soviet press officer at the UN, was reported to have told an American official that evening: "This could well be our last conversation. . . . New York will be blown up tomorrow by Soviet nuclear weapons."

WEDNESDAY, OCTOBER 24

On Wednesday morning the crisis over Cuba intensified dramatically. For the first time ever, the U.S. Strategic Air Command moved its alert posture to DEFCON 2, just one step removed from war (DEFCON 1). Not only senior officials felt the tension; frayed nerves appeared among the public in the United States and elsewhere. In Moscow a group of youngsters vented their anxiety by splashing the American embassy with ink.

The two superpowers seemed to be stumbling toward a war on the seas. The U.S. blockade of Cuba took effect at 10 a.m. Wednesday—the same time that ExComm officials assembled in the White House for their morning meeting. Shortly after ten, McNamara informed his colleagues that two Soviet vessels, the *Komiles* and the *Gagarin*, were approaching the quarantine line five hundred miles from Cuba, and others were in the vicinity. Then came news that a Russian submarine had positioned itself between the *Komiles* and the *Gagarin*. This complicated matters because the intention had been to use an American cruiser to intercept the ships. With a submarine close by, this procedure would be too dangerous. It was therefore decided to send in an aircraft carrier and helicopters equipped with antisubmarine equipment. The record for this meeting reveals the concern generated by the presence of the Soviet submarine: "There was discussion of the problem of dealing with such submarines, and it was understood that in the event of intervention by a submarine in the process of interception the submarine might have to be destroyed."

ExComm officials waited tensely for news, aware that what every informed citizen had been dreading since 1945, a Soviet-American military engagement that might lead to a nuclear nightmare, now seemed frighteningly imminent. Given the ultimate responsibility that was his, no American policymaker could have been more aware of this than the president. Robert Kennedy later recalled his brother's state of mind and body language in ExComm that morning:.

> I think these few minutes were the time of gravest concern for the President. Was the world on the brink of a holocaust? Was it our error? A mistake? Was there something further that should have been done? Or not done? His hand went up to his face and covered his mouth. He opened and closed his fist. His face seemed drawn, his eyes pained, almost gray. We stared at each other across the table. For a few fleeting seconds, it was almost as though no one else was there and he was no longer the President.

Suddenly an official brought a message to McCone. A number of Soviet ships, the CIA director announced, had stopped dead in the water. This was the occasion for Rusk's memorable aside to Bundy: "We're eyeball to eyeball and I think the other fellow just blinked." Soon news arrived confirming the initial report. Russian ships were either motionless or on their way back to the Soviet Union. War had been averted—at least for the time being. American policymakers were not the only ones who felt the tension ease. Officials at the Soviet embassy in Washington greeted the news with a palpable sigh of relief.

Kennedy decided to match the caution Khrushchev had displayed that morning. He immediately instructed the navy to avoid intercepting any Russian ship for at least an hour. That would allow ample time for those vessels with orders to turn around to do so, as well as an opportunity to collect more information on what had taken place. Kennedy also resisted pressure from his advisers to stop the *Bucharest*, a Soviet tanker that had been allowed to pass through the quarantine line. Some ExComm officials thought this was a good opportunity to show Khrushchev the extent of their determination to prevail in this confrontation. As the ship was almost certainly carrying no military equipment, however, the president felt there was no need to stop it. In the end, the *Bucharest* was allowed to proceed to Cuba.

More than just acting to ensure that the crisis did not spin out of control, the Kennedy administration now began to consider steps that would end it. Since October 18 the president and his advisers had recognized that the Jupiter missiles in Turkey might have to be withdrawn if a settlement were to be reached. Interest in a trade had somewhat diminished once the crisis became a public affair. Any sort of deal on the Jupiters would imply a reasonable comparison between those weapons and the missiles in Cuba—and that would undermine the administration's public position that the Soviet deployment of nuclear weapons in Cuba was intolerable. Still, beginning on October 24, the Kennedy team began to focus on ways in which the Jupiters could help end the crisis.

The State Department officials who the day before had sketched out a possible diplomatic settlement involving the Jupiters polished their recommendations on Wednesday in a memorandum to Rusk. They argued that the Turks and the Italians might be persuaded to announce the withdrawal of the missiles from their countries if a commitment were made to guarantee their protection in the short term with Polaris submarines and in the long term with a multilateral sea-based force "in whose ownership, manning, and control they can actively participate."

George Ball sent a cable to Raymond Hare and Thomas Finletter, the American ambassadors to Turkey and NATO, respectively, informing them that the administration was considering a deal on the Jupiters. A negotiated settlement to the crisis, Ball explained, might "involve [the] dismantling and removal" of the missiles in Turkey. He asked Hare and Finletter for their opinions on the political consequences of withdrawing the Jupiters. Over the next few days the Jupiter issue became ever more intertwined with the effort to achieve a diplomatic solution to the crisis.

For Khrushchev this was a period of considerable frustration. True, he could take comfort from an upbeat report on the outlook of the Soviet military. "All servicemen passionately approve of the policies of the USSR government," gushed two aides. "[They] express readiness to fulfill without delay every order of the Motherland aimed at the crushing defeat of the American aggressors." Nonetheless the main development on Wednesday was that Khrushchev had been forced to respect the blockade. Round one had gone to Kennedy.

The Soviet leader betrayed signs of his frustration in the letter he sent to JFK that day. "You, Mr. President, have flung a challenge at us," he declared. "Who asked you to do this? By what right did you do this?" Khrushchev went on to argue that Kennedy had no right to establish the blockade, that OAS support for the quarantine was irrelevant, and that JFK had taken a tough stance on Cuba in part to bolster the Democratic party's chances in the congressional elections. Concluding, he warned that "the Soviet Government cannot instruct the captains of Soviet vessels bound for Cuba to observe the orders of American naval forces blockading that Island"— though his actions in respecting the quarantine that morning did not square with this statement. In a meeting that day with U.S. businessman William Knox, and in a message he dispatched to British philosopher Bertrand Russell, Khrushchev expressed his displeasure with equal force.

Thursday, October 25

Kennedy provided a stout defense of the American position in the letter he sent Thursday in response to Khrushchev's message. "I regret very much that you still do not appear to understand what it is that has moved us in this matter." "The sequence of events is clear," he went on to explain. Reports of a military buildup in Cuba in August had prompted him to say publicly that he would not permit the delivery of offensive weapons to that island. Following that announcement, Soviet officials informed the Kennedy administration that no such missiles were being sent to the Caribbean. Having received those assurances, the president had "urged restraint" upon the hawks in the United States who were demanding forceful action against Cuba. Then he learned that the Soviet Union was placing missiles in Cuba. "I ask you to recognize clearly, Mr. Chairman," Kennedy wrote, "that it was not I who issued the first challenge in this case, and that in the light of this record these activities in Cuba required the responses I have announced."

While Kennedy provided no indication in his correspondence with Khrushchev that he might consider approaches other than the blockade to settle the crisis, in his talks with advisers that was not the case. At the morning ExComm session he asked for the preparation of "alternative courses of action." When ExComm reconvened in the afternoon, drafts of scenarios for three options—an air strike on Cuba, a political path leading to a negotiated settlement, and an intensified blockade—were considered.

A group led by Douglas Dillon wrote the draft for the air attack. An air strike would be preceded by a series of steps, such as a White House statement, an evacuation warning to the population in areas to be attacked, and a letter to Khrushchev as the strike began, and would be followed by a range of actions that included a major presidential address and a report to the UN Security Council and the OAS.

Walt Rostow put together the memorandum on extending the blockade. In it he stressed the vulnerability of the Cuban economy to a quarantine that denied petroleum, oil, and lubricants (POL) as well as weapons. Cuba was totally dependent on imports of POL, Rostow explained, hence blockading those goods could bring the Cuban economy to a standstill within six months. Extending the blockade to POL also kept future options open. Military or diplomatic alternatives would still be viable.

The diplomatic alternative centered on the Jupiters in Turkey. It was not only American officials who explored this approach on October 25; there was widespread talk of a Turkey-for-Cuba missile swap. Walter Lippmann proposed a trade along those lines in his syndicated column. Austrian Foreign Minister Bruno Kreisky did likewise at a political rally in Vienna. The Soviet ambassador in Ankara, Nikita Ryzhov, decided to see the Turkish foreign minister, apparently on his own initiative, to persuade him to encourage his government to agree to any settlement involving the withdrawal of missiles from Cuba and Turkey.

Publicly at least, the Kennedy administration's position was that a Cuba-for-Turkey swap was not viable. Rusk told journalists precisely that at a State Department briefing. Even in private, U.S. officials did not unanimously favor a trade. Finletter, for example, sent a cable to the State Department explaining his own misgivings about a deal on the Jupiters, as well as those of the Turkish representative to NATO.

Among the American officials who were interested in a Jupiter trade, it was Llewellyn Thompson who spearheaded the effort to examine this diplomatic alternative. In a memorandum entitled "Political Path," a number of approaches were discussed: a summit meeting, talks at the UN, a private approach to Castro. The Jupiters in Turkey, however, were seen as a likely focus for negotiations. A straight swap of the nuclear weapons in Cuba and Turkey was mentioned, as was the idea of sending UN inspection teams to the missile sites in those countries. These were the two strategies that ExComm officials had considered three days before.

In that earlier meeting Kennedy had argued that the inspection proposal should be regarded as the appropriate first step in any effort to use the Jupiters to defuse the crisis. A Cuba-for-Turkey missile trade would be the second step. Evidence suggests that by October 25 Kennedy was already setting the wheels in motion for the implementation of an inspection plan. In a telegram sent in the late afternoon, the British representative to the UN reported to his superiors in London that "a most reliable source" had informed him of comments made by Andrew Cordier of Columbia University to the effect that "if a United Nations Commission could be introduced to keep a watch on Russian bases in Cuba under satisfactory guarantees, the United States might be prepared to consider allowing a similar United Nations Commission to look at some bases elsewhere, e.g. the United States bases in Turkey." It seems that by October 25, then, Kennedy had begun to factor the Jupiters in Turkey into a possible diplomatic settlement of the crisis.

As the Kennedy administration considered its options in private, Soviet-American differences over Cuba were being aired publicly and acrimoniously in the United Nations. In a televised late-afternoon meeting of the Security Council, Adlai Stevenson squared off against Soviet Ambassador to the UN Valerian A. Zorin. Stevenson did not pull his punches:

STEVENSON: Do you, Ambassador Zorin, deny that the U.S.S.R. has placed, and is placing medium and intermediate-range missiles and sites in Cuba? Yes or no? Don't wait for the translation, yes or no?

ZORIN: I am not in an American courtroom, sir, and therefore I do not wish to answer a question that is put to me in the fashion in which a prosecutor puts questions. In due course, sir, you will have your answer.

STEVENSON: You are in the courtroom of world opinion right now, and you can answer yes or no. You have denied that they exist, and I want to know whether I have understood you correctly.

ZORIN: Continue with your statement. You will have your answer in due course.

STEVENSON: I am prepared to wait for my answer until hell freezes over, if that's your decision. And I am also prepared to present the evidence in this room.

True to his word, Stevenson showed the Security Council the photographs that proved the existence of the missile sites in Cuba. In his report to the Soviet Ministry of Foreign Affairs, Zorin claimed that "The attempts of the USA representative to turn the Council into a tribune for base propaganda met no support from other members of the Council." But it was clear that Stevenson had won the encounter on points, if not by a knockout.

As secretary general to the UN, U Thant felt a special responsibility to do all he could to end the missile crisis, or at least to prevent it from spiraling out of control. After receiving a positive response from Khrushchev but a more equivocal one from Kennedy to his suggestion that the United States suspend the blockade and the Soviet Union stop shipping weapons to Cuba, he sent fresh proposals on October 25. This time he asked Khrushchev to make sure his vessels stayed away from the blockade line, and he encouraged Kennedy to avoid a clash with Soviet ships for a few days in order to allow time to forge a peaceful settlement. Khrushchev and Kennedy agreed.

Dobrynin and his colleagues in the Soviet embassy continued to keep a watchful eye on developments in the United States. In a cable sent to Moscow that day, the embassy passed on the gist of American press accounts that said Kennedy was contemplating an air strike on the missile sites in Cuba. Acknowledging that these stories might have been manufactured to put additional pressure on Moscow, embassy officials tended to believe them nonetheless. "We cannot entirely rule out," they warned, "above all if we take account of his entourage, the possibility of his making such reckless moves as a bombing raid on the Cuban missile bases or even an invasion of Cuba although this is clearly less likely." This ominous embassy report may have played a role in shaping the letter Khrushchev sent to Kennedy the next day.

On the evening of October 25 American vessels permitted an East German passenger ship, the *Volker Freundschaft*, to pass through the blockade line. In many ways the caution Kennedy displayed on this matter illustrated the prudence both he and Khrushchev had shown since October 22. Despite the skill and good sense they had demonstrated in avoiding a direct military confrontation, however, neither leader had thus far been prepared to offer a realistic diplomatic settlement involving mutual concessions. Even Kennedy's probable behind-the-scenes maneuvering on the Jupiters would not in itself have ended the crisis. Inspection teams would have made it more difficult for Kennedy to strike Cuba and for Khrushchev to attack Turkey, but this would not have constituted a permanent settlement. For the Kennedy administration, the essential element in any agreement was removal of the nuclear weapons from Cuba.

FRIDAY, OCTOBER 26

Early Friday morning the *Marucla* became the first Soviet vessel to be stopped and boarded by the U.S. navy. The Russians did not retaliate. For Kennedy, this was a positive step: a determination to enforce the blockade had been displayed, but the non-Soviet origins of the ship—it was Panamanian-owned and had been registered in Lebanon—ensured that its interception did not incense Khrushchev.

That morning's ExComm session soon turned to a discussion of the options available if the blockade alone failed to bring about a withdrawal of the missiles from Cuba. As always, the military alternatives were understood. But Ex-Comm officials must have been sobered by McNamara's report that the military expected casualties in an invasion of Cuba to be very heavy. (It was estimated a few days later that close to twenty thousand Americans might be killed in the first ten days of fighting.) "We are going to have to face the fact," Kennedy reflected, "that, if we do invade, by the time we get to these sites, after a very bloody fight, they will be pointed at us. And we must further accept the possibility that when military hostilities first begin, those missiles will be fired."

The extension of the blockade to POL was another alternative that received much attention, with a number of officials calling for its implementation either immediately or in the next day or two. In the end it was agreed to delay a decision on POL until the direction of political talks, including negotiations at the UN, had been determined.

Adlai Stevenson, for his part, introduced into the discussion the possibility of a diplomatic settlement that included significant American concessions. Thus he returned to the approach he had advocated during the first week of the crisis. As quid pro quo for the withdrawal of the missiles from Cuba, Stevenson predicted, "the Russians would ask us for a new guarantee of the territorial integrity of Cuba and the dismantlement of U.S. strategic missiles in Turkey." The hawkish McCone wasted no time in attacking Stevenson, arguing that the missiles in Turkey and Cuba should not be linked. "The Soviet weapons in Cuba were pointed at our heart," the CIA director added, "and put us under great handicap in continuing to carry out our commitments to the free world." McCone's assault was effective; discussion of the issues that Stevenson had raised soon fizzled.

Kennedy meanwhile gave the impression of a leader intent on keeping his options open. "We will get the Soviet strategic missiles out of Cuba only by invading Cuba or by trading," he stated, thereby revealing that for him both the military and diplomatic approaches were important alternatives. Kennedy also seems to have had an open mind about extending the blockade to POL, although the above remark replies that he regarded it as a sensible intermediary step rather than a strategy that could effect the removal of the missiles from Cuba.

Although JFK recognized on Friday that diplomacy was a key option, he felt that some concessions could be made more easily to the Soviets than others. Specifically he believed that offering to remove the Jupiter missiles from Turkey was more acceptable from the American point of view than promising never to invade Cuba. His comment that the crisis could be resolved "only by invading Cuba or by trading" suggests that he felt a deal on the Jupiters was feasible. But it did not indicate a willingness to incorporate a no-invasion pledge into any diplomatic settlement. Kennedy tackled this subject more directly in discussing a Brazilian plan to bar all nuclear weapons from Latin America, including those in Cuba. The problem with the Brazilian proposal, he argued, was that it also called for "a guarantee of the territorial integrity of all Latin American states. He asked whether we could commit ourselves not to invade Cuba." Kennedy's comments in ExComm on October 26 demonstrate the influence that early assumptions about policy toward Cuba still had on his thinking, namely that the use of force to overthrow Castro was an essential policy option.

It was on Friday afternoon that ABC reporter John Scali and a KGB officer in Washington, Aleksandr Feklisov (alias Fomin), began to play a role that neither Soviet nor American leaders had planned. They were unlikely participants in a major international crisis, but both appear to have been genuinely moved by the terror of the situation. Following a call from Feklisov, the two men met for lunch at a Washington restaurant where they discussed a three-point plan to defuse the crisis: Khrushchev would consent to the removal of the missiles from Cuba under UN supervision; Castro would agree never to receive such weapons again; and Kennedy would pledge not to invade Cuba. This episode has sparked controversy. According to the notes Scali took at the time, as well as his later comments, the plan was advanced by Feklisov. But Feklisov's telegrams to Moscow at the time, as well as his subsequent reflections, indicated that Scali had made these proposals.

What is certain is the enthusiasm with which State Department officials greeted Scali's report on his meeting with Feklisov. Despite the no-invasion pledge, Rusk thought the proposals were good ones, and he asked the reporter to arrange another rendezvous in order to communicate the administration's interest. Hence Scali contacted Feklisov and arranged an early evening meeting at a Washington hotel. In a brief conversation, Scali told the KGB agent that he had been authorized to say there were "real possibilities in this [proposal]" and that Soviet and American representatives could work on it at the UN with the help of U Thant.

Only after this second meeting did Feklisov report these events to KGB headquarters. That message did not arrive in Moscow until Saturday afternoon, October 27 (Moscow time), and it was another four hours before the KGB sent it to Foreign Minister Gromyko. This means that Khrushchev would have known nothing of Feklisov's contacts with Scali until after composing and dispatching not only his October 26 letter to Kennedy, but his message on the 27th as well.

While the Scali-Feklisov dialogue did not affect Khrushchev's strategy on Friday or Saturday, it did shape the Kennedy administration's thinking. This was because American officials erroneously assumed that Feklisov had been doing Khrushchev's bidding—and therefore that his proposals were important ones. This supposition caused the Kennedy administration to link the Feklisov initiative to the long, now famous letter that Khrushchev sent to Kennedy on Friday evening, October 26.

Stripped of the usual formalities of diplomatic correspondence, the Soviet leader bared his soul in a message that was philosophical and deeply emotional. He spoke of his fear of a superpower military engagement: "...should war indeed break out, it would not be in our power to contain or stop it, for such is the logic of war. I have taken part in two wars, and I know that war ends only when it has rolled through cities and villages, sowing death and destruction everywhere." He

went on to argue that the weapons in Cuba were intended
only to defend the island from attack, that the Soviet state was
committed to peaceful coexistence with the West, and that the
blockade was unacceptably provocative.

Toward the end of his message Khrushchev sketched the
outlines of a possible settlement. If Kennedy promised not to
attack Cuba, restrained others from doing so, and ended the
quarantine,

> this would immediately change everything. I do not speak
> for Fidel Castro, but I think that he and the Government of
> Cuba would, probably, announce a demobilization and
> would call upon the people to commence peaceful work.
> Then the question of armaments would also be obviated,
> because when there is no threat, armaments are only a bur-
> den for any people. This would also change the approach
> to the question of destroying not only the armaments
> which you call offensive, but of every other kind of arma-
> ment.

The basic deal that Khrushchev seemed to be offering
Kennedy was removal of the missiles in exchange for a no-
invasion pledge. Later in his message, the Soviet premier
muddied the waters by saying that an American commitment
not to invade Cuba would obviate "the necessity for the presence of our military specialists in Cuba," without mentioning
the presence of nuclear weapons. Still, Khrushchev's message
could be viewed as an offer of a settlement to end the crisis,
the basic components of which were an American no-invasion
pledge and the withdrawal of Soviet missiles from Cuba.
When they examined Khrushchev's message alongside the
offer they believed Feklisov had made to Scali on behalf of the
Soviet leader, that is how Kennedy and his advisers inter-

preted it. They asked the State Department to evaluate the Soviet leader's letter by the following day.

Some have suggested that the emotion suffusing Khrushchev's October 26 message was the sign of a man either
drunk or wilting under pressure. The Soviet leader's letter
was in fact a brave and vitally important contribution to the
resolution of the missile crisis. For the confrontation to be
brought to an end peaceably, either Kennedy or Khrushchev
had to be the first to propose a settlement based on mutual
concessions, and to be willing, therefore, to run the risk of losing face, of being ridiculed for backing down in a major cold
war crisis. To Khrushchev's credit, he was prepared to take this
risk. The earnestness of his letter should be regarded as the
commendably fervent desire of a leader, aware of his responsibilities, to end a crisis that he found unsettlingly dangerous.

As Kennedy considered his options on Friday and Khrushchev proposed terms for a settlement, Castro prepared for
war. By this point he was convinced that an American attack
was inevitable and close at hand. "On the night of the 26th,"
Castro recalled in 1992, "we saw no possible solution. We
couldn't see a way out. Under the threat of an invasion, of an
attack, with enormous propaganda using all the mass media,
and an international campaign talking about this very serious
problem, we really couldn't see any solution." Castro therefore
decided to take preliminary action, ordering his anti-aircraft
forces to fire at low-flying American planes.

Soviet commanders and troops in Cuba were also bracing
themselves for war, certain that an American assault would
come, perhaps as early as the next day. Following an old Russian tradition that soldiers bathe before battle—"a sort of rit-
ual purification," as one official later put it—Soviet troops in
Cuba showered or swam regularly during this period. Soviet

military commanders agreed that any American attack would soon overwhelm them, but they were determined that an initial defeat of this sort would not end matters. Any survivors, it was decided, would escape into the interior of the island, where they would fight as a guerrilla force alongside their Cuban allies. If Kennedy decided to invade Cuba, he could expect a long, bloody struggle to subdue the island.

SATURDAY, OCTOBER 27

After midnight: Fidel Castro dictated a letter to Khrushchev in the early hours of Saturday from the Soviet embassy in Havana. Convinced that an American attack would soon imperil his beloved revolution, the Cuban leader now turned to alarming options. "From an analysis of the situation and the reports in our possession," Castro informed Khrushchev, "I consider that the aggression [from the U.S.] is almost imminent within the next 24 or 72 hours." An air strike was the most likely form of attack, but an invasion could not be ruled out. If the United States did invade Cuba, "that would be the moment to eliminate such danger forever through an act of clear legitimate defense, however harsh and terrible the solution would be, for there is no other." In other words, Khrushchev should respond to an invasion of Cuba by authorizing a nuclear strike against the United States. It was almost dawn when Castro finished his letter. The Soviet leader probably did not receive it until the night of October 27-28 (Moscow time).

9 a.m.: Radio Moscow began broadcasting a message from Khrushchev to Kennedy. After once again asserting that the missiles had been sent to defend Cuba, not to threaten the United States, Khrushchev noted the double standard in

American objections to the presence of missiles in the Caribbean.

> You are disturbed over Cuba. You say that this disturbs you because it is 90 miles by sea from the coast of the United States of America. But Turkey adjoins us; our sentries patrol back and forth and see each other. Do you consider, then, that you have the right to demand security for your own country and the removal of the weapons you call offensive, but do not accord the same right to us? You have placed destructive missile weapons, which you call offensive, in Turkey, literally next to us. How then can recognition of our equal military capacities be reconciled with such unequal relations between our great states? This is irreconcilable.

Changing the deal offered the previous day, Khrushchev now suggested that Kennedy take the Jupiters out of Turkey and promise not to invade Cuba; in turn he would remove Soviet missiles from Cuba and agree not to attack Turkey. Both missile withdrawals would take place under UN inspection, providing the Turkish and Cuban governments did not object. Released in public, Khrushchev's message was aimed not only at offering a way out of the crisis but at influencing world opinion. "Why would I like to do this?" he asked. "Because the whole world is now apprehensive and expects sensible actions by us. The greatest joy for all peoples would be the announcement of our agreement and of the eradication of the controversy that has arisen."

Why Khrushchev decided to offer JFK this deal—demanding the removal of the Jupiters from Turkey after making no reference to them in his message the previous evening—remains a mystery. Having sent his October 26 letter, he may have received information from Soviet intelligence that a U.S. attack on Cuba was less imminent than previously assumed; and that may have encouraged him to seek an additional concession from Kennedy. Alternatively, Khrushchev may have regarded Walter Lippmann's October 25 newspaper article suggesting the idea of a Turkey-Cuba missile trade as a trial balloon put up by the Kennedy administration.

10 a.m.: ExComm officials met in the White House. Their most important task was to make sense of the two different sets of proposals made by Khrushchev within the past sixteen hours, and to formulate an effective response to them. Developments in the next few hours would make their work even more difficult.

10:15 to 11 a.m.: An American U-2 plane strayed off course into Soviet airspace over Chukotski Peninsula during what was apparently a routine air-sampling mission. When Soviet MiG planes took off to intercept the U-2, it seemed that a Soviet-American clash might be caused inadvertently. The U-2, however, managed to leave Soviet airspace before shots were fired. "There is always some son of a bitch who doesn't get the word," Kennedy remarked on learning of the incident.

Around 12 noon: Even more disturbing than this U-2 episode was one that occurred later over Cuba. Influenced by the decision of the Cubans to begin firing on low-flying American planes, a Soviet military commander took it upon himself to order a surface-to-air missile attack on an approaching American U-2. The order was carried out, the plane downed, and the pilot, Major Rudolf Anderson, killed. To many ExComm officials, the incident seemed a clear indication that the Soviets were intent on escalating the crisis.

This development was only one of several issues explored by Kennedy and his ExComm colleagues on Saturday. Their first order of business was to prepare a response to Khrushchev's October 26 and 27 messages.

Kennedy remained reluctant to offer assurances against an invasion of Cuba, a concession demanded by Khrushchev in both his letters. Looking at the situation long term, the president was more concerned about making a commitment that would ensure Castro remained in power than agreeing to remove obsolete missiles from Turkey that he had been interested in removing anyway. "There are disadvantages" in the October 26 Soviet offer, Kennedy declared in ExComm, because it implied "a guarantee of Cuba." Others in the administration shared JFK's concern. An October 27 State Department memorandum, for example, asked in connection with the previous day's Khrushchev/Feklisov initiatives: "Is it politically feasible for the US in effect to guarantee the permanence of the Castro regime?"

This was part of the dubious legacy of earlier policy thinking on Cuba—the unchallenged assumption that Castro must be overthrown and that the use of force against Cuba was thus an important policy option. In the context of the missile crisis, this idea was a dangerous impediment to the peace process. In the end Kennedy accepted the obvious—that preventing war was more important than retaining the alternative of military action against Castro.

The strategy adopted by the president and his advisers was to disregard Khrushchev's second letter but to respond enthusiastically to the first, making clear that the United States was willing to offer assurances against an invasion of Cuba. This approach ensured that trading the Jupiters in Turkey did not become a part of the formal settlement of the missile crisis. (Developments later in the day showed that JFK did not mind incorporating the Jupiters informally into the settlement.)

Thirteen Days, Robert Kennedy's memoir of the crisis, has traditionally shaped our understanding of the process by which this strategy was formulated. In it, Robert Kennedy wrote: "I suggested, and was supported by Ted Sorensen and others, that we ignore the latest Khrushchev offer and respond to his earlier letter's proposal, as refined in the offer made to John Scali."

Historians perhaps should have been skeptical of the account that it was Robert Kennedy (with Sorensen's assistance) who thought of the tactic that ultimately ended the missile crisis. Those who advanced this account, after all, were Robert Kennedy and, as we learned in 1989, close aide Ted Sorensen, who had edited *Thirteen Days*. A close reading of the records of the October 27 ExComm meetings shows that the attorney general did not devise the plan to respond only to Khrushchev's October 26 message. A number of officials first recommended that approach, including Paul Nitze (at least implicitly), McGeorge Bundy, Sorensen, and Stevenson. Bundy, for instance, advised JFK to "answer back saying I would prefer to deal . . . with your interesting proposals of last night." After seriously considering Khrushchev's October 27 offer, Robert Kennedy came around to the same position, and his advice was important in convincing the president of the soundness of this approach. Still, Robert Kennedy did not introduce the tactic that defused the missile crisis; it was a team effort.

As well as deciding on a response to Khrushchev's messages, the president and his advisers needed to consider what they would do if the Soviet leader rejected their acceptance of the deal offered in his October 26 letter. On this issue the president was suitably cautious. In the comments he made to his ExComm colleagues, Kennedy now argued that the use of force against Cuba, the alternative favored by his military advisers, should be viewed as the option of last resort. Two other approaches should be tried first. One was to encourage Turkey and other NATO partners to propose publicly a Cuba-for-Turkey missile trade that the Kennedy administration would then accept. By saying an American attack on Cuba that might cause Soviet retaliation in Berlin and Turkey was imminent, and by promising that Polaris submarines would be deployed in the Mediterranean to protect Turkey if the Jupiters were withdrawn, the administration might be able to persuade NATO to go along with this. And, Kennedy added, it would be far better for U.S. credibility if the proposal were to come from NATO than from Washington. The trade would then look less like an American concession.

The second step Kennedy favored before taking military action was the addition of POL to the items being intercepted by the blockade. Many of the president's advisers also favored extending the blockade in this way. Given the president's line of thinking in ExComm on Saturday, a Khrushchev rejection of Kennedy's acceptance of the October 26 offer would probably not have led immediately to an American attack on Cuba and thus to war.

What made that rejection less likely was the outcome of a discussion that took place between Kennedy and a group of senior officials outside of ExComm in the late afternoon. On Rusk's advice, the president asked his brother to call Ambassador Dobrynin to set up a meeting. Robert Kennedy was authorized to say that the Jupiters would be taken out of Turkey in the near future, but that this development could not be incorporated into a formal, public settlement of the missile crisis. JFK's position was that a Turkey-for-Cuba missile trade was basically fair and feasible, but that it would be perceived, particularly by America's NATO partners, as a U.S. concession to Soviet pressure. As he saw it, the Robert Kennedy–

Dobrynin channel could solve that problem. The promise to remove the Jupiters could be made to Dobrynin, hence an added inducement for Khrushchev to remove the missiles from Cuba would be provided. But the negative consequences of a public trade would be avoided.

4:15 p.m.: Following a request from Rusk, Scali organized another meeting with Feklisov. Scali, who had been enraged by Khrushchev's new offer earlier in the day, did not mince his words. Bringing the Jupiters into the equation was a "stinking double cross," he bellowed; consequently an American attack was but a few hours away. Feklisov insisted there had been a communications problem. Khrushchev, he said, had sent the October 27 message before receiving his cable reporting the positive American reaction to his October 26 offer. After the meeting, Scali typed out a memorandum of his talk with Feklisov that was immediately circulated to ExComm officials.

7:45 p.m.: Dobrynin arrived at Robert Kennedy's office in the Justice Department, following a phone call from the attorney general. During their conversation the attorney general used intimidation and inducement as ways of bolstering Soviet willingness to end the crisis. On the one hand, he stressed the seriousness of the situation. The downing of the U-2 plane had startled American officials, and military advisers were urging the president to use force; so Soviet accommodation was needed within the next twenty-four hours in order to prevent an attack on Cuba. On the other hand, he explained that the president was confident Khrushchev's October 26 letter could form the basis of a settlement. The Kennedy administration was prepared to offer assurances that there would be no invasion of Cuba, as Khrushchev had requested. In addition, his brother intended to remove the Jupiter missiles from Turkey once the Cuban crisis had been defused. This part of the deal had to remain private. If the Soviets mentioned it in public, the trade would be off.

Dobrynin, for his part, was struck not only by Robert Kennedy's comments but by his demeanor. In the cable he sent to Moscow that same evening, he described the attorney general as "very upset; in any case, I've never seen him like this before. . . . He didn't even try to get into fights on various subjects, as he usually does, and only persistently returned to one topic: time is of the essence and we shouldn't miss the chance."

JFK's use of secret diplomacy through the Robert Kennedy–Dobrynin channel may well have been only one part of a two-pronged maneuver on the Jupiters that evening. According to Rusk's 1987 recollections, the president asked him to dictate over the phone to Andrew Cordier of Columbia University a statement to be made by U Thant calling for the removal of the missiles from Turkey and Cuba. Cordier was to deliver the statement to U Thant on a moment's notice.

Kennedy, then, probably decided on Saturday evening to accept—or at least to give himself the option of accepting—a public deal on the Jupiters in the event Khrushchev decided against a private Jupiter trade, providing the public agreement appeared to originate in the UN rather than in his administration. This Cordier ploy would have represented a revised version of the inspection-team plan that had been hatched on or around October 25. It is possible but less likely, however, that Rusk, who thus far remains the only source for this part of the story on October 27, misremembered the events of Saturday evening. The Cordier ploy as he recalled it may never have existed.

8:05 p.m.: JFK's letter to Khrushchev, calling for a settlement "along the lines suggested in your letter of October 26," was sent to Moscow and released simultaneously to the press. Soviet missiles would be withdrawn from Cuba under UN inspection, the blockade would end, and the United States (and other nations in the Western Hemisphere) would promise not to invade Cuba. By dispatching this letter and sending his brother to see Dobrynin, Kennedy had, by Saturday evening, returned the ball to Khrushchev's court. The critical question now was, how would he respond?

Late evening (Moscow time): A cluster of developments, beginning in the evening and continuing the next morning, convinced Khrushchev that the crisis was getting out of hand and that a settlement needed to be reached quickly. The shooting down of the U-2 plane over Cuba, an action he had not sanctioned, reminded him that an incident beyond his control might trigger a major conflict. Reports from his own intelligence services that an American attack on Cuba "was being prepared and that an invasion would probably be unavoidable unless we came to an agreement with the president" alarmed him. And the letter from Castro "added fuel," as one adviser recalls, "to the anxious thoughts preying on his mind." Castro's message troubled Khrushchev on two counts. First, it reinforced the information he was receiving from his own intelligence sources, namely that Kennedy would soon authorize military action against Cuba. Second, Castro's suggestion that Khrushchev respond to an invasion of Cuba with a nuclear strike against the United States indicated that his key ally in this confrontation was losing his cool.

The tension of the Cuban missile crisis peaked that Saturday evening. Only those who lived through that time, and particularly those with the responsibility for the outcome of events, can truly appreciate the profound sense of fear created by the world's most dangerous crisis. "I remember leaving the White House at the end of that Saturday," a tearful Robert McNamara once recalled. "It was a beautiful fall day; and [I remember] thinking that might well be the last sunset I saw."

SUNDAY, OCTOBER 28

Morning-afternoon (Moscow time): Khrushchev called a morning meeting of his senior advisers. The mood was somber and tense. "From the outset the participants were on edge," recalls one official. "Practically only Khrushchev spoke, with Anastas Mikoyan and Andrei Gromyko contributing some remarks. Others preferred to keep silent as if hinting to Khrushchev that since he had made his bed he could sleep on it."

By the time the meeting started, Kennedy's October 27 message, offering a no-invasion pledge in return for the withdrawal of the missiles from Cuba, had been received. Dobrynin's report on his talk with Robert Kennedy arrived later. Its essentials—that the Jupiters could be removed from Turkey by secret agreement, that the American military was urging the president to order an attack on Cuba, and that Khrushchev needed to act quickly to bring about a peaceful settlement to the crisis—were immediately grasped. Misinformation also played a role in shaping Khrushchev's outlook. General Semyon Ivanov was called away to take a phone call. On his return he announced that Kennedy was set to address the American people later in the day. The assumption among officials at the meeting was that JFK would use the speech to announce military action against Cuba. Ivanov's information about a presidential address was false. Nevertheless it served to strengthen the feeling of Khrushchev and his advisers that a quick settlement must be reached if an American attack on Cuba were to be prevented.

All these developments convinced Khrushchev to accept

the offer Kennedy had made the day before. He persuaded his colleagues that there was no alternative to this course of action, dictated a letter to Kennedy that his advisers then polished, and ordered an aide to deliver the message to Radio Moscow for immediate broadcast. The aide sped through the city, ignoring traffic regulations to make sure the message was transmitted as soon as possible.

Khrushchev meanwhile composed a letter to Castro. He asked his ally to stay calm (good advice, for the Cuban leader was enraged by the news that Khrushchev had agreed to remove the missiles) and implored him to view the settlement as a positive development: the American no-invasion pledge would guarantee Cuban security. Gromyko dispatched a telegram to Dobrynin, instructing him to arrange another meeting with Robert Kennedy. Dobrynin was to inform the attorney general that Khrushchev had sent a message to JFK promising to withdraw the missiles from Cuba.

9 a.m. (Washington time): Radio Moscow began to broadcast Khrushchev's message to Kennedy. The Soviet leader reported that he had "issued a new order on the dismantling of the weapons which you describe as 'offensive,' and their crating and return to the Soviet Union." "I regard with respect and trust," he went on to say, "your statement in your message of October 27, 1962 that no attack will be made on Cuba." Khrushchev did not refer to the missiles in Turkey.

11 a.m. (Washington time): Elated ExComm officials gathered to reflect on the morning's developments. The tension of the previous few days had evaporated. There was "an exhilarating atmosphere," recalls Kennedy aide Don Wilson. "I think every man in that room felt exactly the same—that the curtains had lifted—because only 24 hours before it looked so dark." President Kennedy himself was "in great form. . . . He was smiling and he was full of humor and he, too, had obviously felt a great burden lift." "It was a marvelous morning," Wilson adds. "I'll never forget it as long as I live."

In that ExComm meeting Kennedy began the process of tying up loose ends. A letter was written and sent to Khrushchev later in the day. "I consider my letter to you of October twenty-seventh and your reply of today," JFK told the Soviet leader in that message, "as firm undertakings on the part of both our governments which should be promptly carried out." Kennedy also issued a public statement, applauding Khrushchev's "statesmanlike decision" to withdraw the missiles from Cuba. This, JFK acknowledged, was "an important and constructive contribution to peace."

As ExComm officials started their meeting, Robert Kennedy began his with Dobrynin. The Soviet ambassador reiterated that Khrushchev had indeed decided to accept the settlement offered by JFK the previous day. Robert Kennedy reminded Dobrynin that the understanding on the removal of the Jupiters from Turkey must remain secret. In a report sent to Moscow later in the day, Dobrynin emphasized Robert Kennedy's evident relief at the news of Khrushchev's decision. "It looks like this is the first time I can go home feeling at ease," the attorney general had observed, smiling, "knowing that nothing bad can happen to my family." It was a sentiment shared by millions of people throughout the world.

6

Aftermath and Conclusion

IT WAS ONE THING to reach a settlement on Cuba, another to implement it. During November 1962 the major protagonists provided different interpretations of the deal cut on October 27 and 28, then tried to reconcile them. For a time these disputes appeared to jeopardize the peace that Kennedy and Khrushchev had secured. Castro and Kennedy were largely responsible for the tension of this period. The Cuban leader, humiliated by a settlement forged without his participation and entailing the withdrawal of the missiles from his island, was scarcely in an agreeable mood. Kennedy, for his part, sought to define the October 27–28 deal in a way that maximized Soviet and Cuban concessions while minimizing those of the United States. He wanted to enhance his own credibility and maintain the options theoretically available to him for future policy toward Cuba.

Castro supplied an alternative vision of a permanent settlement to the crisis over Cuba as early as October 28. In a message sent to the United Nations, he called for five concessions from Kennedy in addition to the no-invasion pledge and the removal of the blockade. These included an end to the U.S. economic embargo and the return of Guantánamo to the Cuban government. While Castro was powerless to force compliance with these demands, he was able to obstruct

Soviet-American attempts to establish appropriate procedures for monitoring the withdrawal of the missiles. Kennedy had said in his October 27 message to Khrushchev that the removal of the nuclear weapons should take place under UN observation. But Castro refused to give his consent, arguing that the presence of UN officials in his country would be an affront to Cuba's sovereignty and prestige. "Whoever tries to inspect Cuba," he threatened, "must come in battle array." Neither U Thant nor Soviet emissary Anastas Mikoyan could persuade Castro to give ground on this issue. Consequently Khrushchev and Kennedy agreed that departing Soviet ships would expose the missiles on their decks so they could be photographed by American planes.

Castro proved equally obstinate on the question of the IL-28 bombers. Although Kennedy had told his ExComm advisers on October 28 to define the removal of those bombers as an optimal objective rather than an essential component of the settlement on Cuba, this was not the position the president came to adopt. The Soviets, he said in early November, must withdraw the IL-28s as well as the medium- and intermediate-range missiles. Khrushchev was understandably perplexed, describing JFK's stance in a November 11 letter as "incomprehensible." Step by step, however, the Soviet leader moved to meet Kennedy's demands on the IL-28s. Castro was less accommodating, but on November 19 he finally agreed to the withdrawal of the bombers. As all the missile sites in Cuba had been dismantled by this point, Kennedy was able to announce the next day that he would now lift the blockade.

The most controversial issue after October 28 was the American no-invasion pledge. Of course this had been a central component of the original settlement, and Kennedy had agreed in his October 27 letter to make that commitment in return for the removal of the missiles under UN inspection.

The stipulation on inspection, though, meant that JFK could later claim that he was not obliged to rule out a future invasion of Cuba because Castro's refusal to permit UN officials on Cuban soil meant the Soviets had failed to keep their part of the bargain. And this was precisely the argument he now made.

As with much of the Kennedy administration's thinking during the missile crisis, this move illustrated the enduring influence of precrisis assumptions, particularly the idea that the use of force to overthrow Castro should remain an important policy option. On November 7 the State Department Policy Planning Council produced a memorandum calling for "a maximal U.S. strategy ... directed at the elimination ... of the Castro regime." Nine days later another State Department official argued that it would be best if the United States did not have to "commit itself to the preservation of the Castro regime." Put bluntly, many American officials wished to have their cake and eat it too. They wished to bring the missile crisis to a final resolution while reneging on the only concession Kennedy had publicly promised (apart from ending the blockade).

Influenced by his advisers in his correspondence with Khrushchev, Kennedy danced around the issue of the no-invasion pledge with balletic agility. The Soviet premier tried hard to pin the president down. Khrushchev proposed, for example, that the promise not to invade Cuba, along with the other commitments made in the October 27–28 settlement, be detailed in a United Nations document; but he did not succeed. At the November 20 press conference at which he announced the lifting of the blockade, Kennedy was ambiguous on this question. On the one hand, he claimed that "important parts of the understanding of October 27th and 28th remain to be carried out," noting Castro's refusal to allow on-site UN verification. Asked whether he would be prepared to invade Cuba without UN approval, Kennedy insisted that Americans, "of course, keep to ourselves . . . the right to defend our security." On the other hand, he declared that while his administration would continue to combat Cuban subversion, "these policies are very different from any intent to launch a military invasion of the island."

In the end the November dialogue between the two leaders failed to produce a formalized version of the settlement that had been sketched out on October 27–28. While JFK refused to offer a categorical assurance against an invasion of Cuba, the fact that no such attack has taken place—despite the obvious desire of Kennedy and later presidents to oust Castro—seems to indicate that successive administrations have regarded the no-invasion pledge as a binding commitment. This was because the October 27–28 settlement was understood by the American public and the international community to entail a United States commitment not to attack Cuba, regardless of the nature of the November Kennedy-Khrushchev dialogue. So it would have been exceedingly difficult for Kennedy or any other chief executive to have justified such an assault. President Richard Nixon and his adviser Henry Kissinger did assure the Soviets in 1970 that the understanding on the no-invasion pledge was "still in full force," thereby making explicit and unambiguous the commitment that Kennedy had made at the end of the missile crisis.

The private agreement on the Jupiters proved far easier to implement than the public parts of the October 27–28 settlement. McNamara assumed responsibility for the removal of the missiles from Turkey, and on April 25, 1963, he was able to report to Kennedy that "the last Jupiter came down yesterday." As a replacement, a Polaris submarine with sixteen missiles was dispatched to the Mediterranean.

The missile crisis was a volcanic event; even though the eruption over Cuba subsided in November 1962, its effects were felt long after. For Castro, the crisis made him more suspicious not only of the United States but of his Soviet ally too. In terms of the Soviet-American contest, the missile crisis both improved and aggravated relations. The tension generated by the crisis, and the recognition that Washington and Moscow had moved unacceptably close to the brink of nuclear disaster, did produce a mutual desire to reduce cold war tensions. The signing of the Nuclear Test Ban Treaty in the summer of 1963 was the most concrete expression of that desire.

The most eloquent expression of a yearning for calm was Kennedy's speech at American University in June 1963. There he argued that long-term peace was a necessary and rational objective, not the unattainable goal of idealistic dreamers. To think otherwise "leads to the conclusion that war is inevitable—that mankind is doomed—that we are gripped by forces we cannot control." Audaciously Kennedy went on to propose: "Let us re-examine our attitude towards the Soviet Union. . . . No government or social system is so evil that its people must be considered as lacking in virtue," he explained, citing the accomplishments of the Russian people in science and space as well as their heroic sacrifices in World War II. The American view of the cold war also needed to be modified, Kennedy suggested. "We are not engaged in a debate, seeking to pile up debating points. We are not here distributing blame or pointing the finger of judgment. . . . We can seek a relaxation of tensions without relaxing our guard." "Confident and unafraid," the president concluded, "we labor on—not toward a strategy of annihilation but toward a strategy of peace." Khrushchev would later describe the speech as "the best . . . by any President since Roosevelt." More than thirty years later it is difficult to read it without being moved and impressed.

This address was significant not only for its lofty sentiments but for the way it prepared public opinion for tangible actions. In late June Soviet and American officials reached an accord in Geneva setting up a "hot line" between Moscow and Washington. This made possible the sort of instantaneous communication between the superpower leaders that had not been available during the missile crisis. More important, the limited test ban was signed a few weeks later, a landmark agreement that curtailed nuclear testing. In the fall of 1963 there were further signs of a budding détente. Kennedy talked privately of his wish to visit the Soviet Union in the near future, and in an October meeting with Foreign Minister Gromyko he discussed ways of expanding Soviet-American cooperation. A collaborative moon project, increased trade, and mutual defense cuts were among the ideas mentioned. Cuba, to some extent, figured in this mellowing of East-West relations in 1963. Although that summer Kennedy authorized a secret program to carry out sabotage in Cuba, and the CIA continued to devise plots to assassinate Castro, some evidence indicates that the president was considering an accommodation with the Cuban leader shortly before he was killed in Dallas.

The missile crisis also had a salutary effect on U.S. nuclear defense strategy, making it more sensible and less intimidating to the Soviet Union. Before October 1962 Kennedy and McNamara had argued that the need for a U.S. first strike against the Soviet Union could not be altogether ruled out. After the sobering experience of the missile crisis, the doctrine of MAD (mutually assured destruction) was developed, under which U.S. policymakers assumed they would never start a nuclear war. They understood that because the Soviet nuclear force could survive an attack and then carry out a retaliatory

strike, talk of a U.S. first strike was totally unrealistic. Likewise American officials were confident that their own ability
to carry out a massive retaliatory strike would deter the Soviets from initiating a nuclear attack on the United States.

In other ways the consequences of the Cuban missile crisis
were less positive. Perhaps most important, the events of October 1962 bolstered Soviet determination to increase defense
spending, especially on nuclear weapons. Moscow understood
that American strategic superiority accounted in large mea-
sure for Khrushchev's backing down in the crisis, and this
recognition encouraged Soviet policymakers to expand their
nuclear arsenal during the remainder of the 1960s. By the
1970s, for the first time in the cold war, the Soviets reached ap-
proximate parity with the United States in nuclear weapons.

The October 1962 crisis may also have contributed to the
deepening of United States involvement in Vietnam. The lesson that some American officials drew from the crisis was that
the gradual escalation of pressure on adversaries worked. The
same approach characterized later American policy in Vietnam: the use of military advisers and special forces in Vietnam
was followed by a massive bombing campaign on Communist
forces, and this in turn led to the decision by President Lyndon Johnson in July 1965 to send large numbers of combat
troops to Southeast Asia. The missile crisis bequeathed to U.S.
policymakers a faith in the strategy of escalation and perhaps a
misplaced belief in their own infallibility, both of which were
called to question in Vietnam.

In addition to its impact on the cold war, the missile crisis
also influenced American political culture. For all those who
had talked about the inherent insanity of the Bomb, the events
of October 1962 became an important reference point, hard
evidence to support the idea that nuclear holocaust was a distinct possibility, not a paranoid vision. If the superpowers had

stumbled toward the brink of war over Cuba, they could do so again; and on a future occasion they might not be as lucky.

Popular culture, too, was affected. Stanley Kubrick's iconoclastic film *Dr. Strangelove, or: How I Learned to Stop Worrying and Love the Bomb* (1964), for example, tells the story of a Soviet-American nuclear crisis. When a deranged anti-Communist general orders a group of B-52s to carry out a nuclear attack on the Soviet Union, the American president, played by Peter Sellers with a look and in a style highly reminiscent of Adlai Stevenson, tries to recall the jets and warns the Russian premier what has happened. Despite his best efforts, one plane proceeds to its target and drops its bombs, an attack that immediately triggers a retaliatory Doomsday device which the Soviets had secretly developed. The film ends apocalyptically with a series of explosions and mushroom clouds. In this brilliant black comedy, Kubrick highlighted the dangers of anti-Communist paranoia as well as the dubious advantages of man's technological achievements. A 1993 light comedy, *Matinee*, tells the story of a maker of horror movies who goes to Florida during the time of the missile crisis to promote his latest film. In a mildly diverting way, *Matinee* captures the sense of tension felt by many Americans in October 1962.

In retrospect, perhaps the most curious and striking aspect of the Cuban crisis was the way the performances of Kennedy and Khrushchev mirrored each other. Both leaders miscalculated the consequences of their policies in 1961 and early 1962. Kennedy failed to consider how policies like the Bay of Pigs, the expulsion of Cuba from the OAS, Operation Mongoose, and increased American defense spending would trouble Khrushchev and Castro, prompting them to take countermeasures. Khrushchev could have devised a far safer plan than putting missiles in Cuba to achieve his foreign policy objectives. Kennedy failed to heed the warnings of those American officials who opposed the Bay of Pigs. Khrushchev likewise ignored those advisers who raised objections to Operation Anadyr.

During the missile crisis itself, the outlook and actions of the two leaders were similar. Kennedy's initial belligerence on October 16 and 17 was followed by a far more moderate, cautious approach which included the implementation of a blockade rather than an air strike and a willingness at the end of the crisis to trade the Jupiters in Turkey. Khrushchev at first talked about disregarding the blockade but proceeded to respect it and, beginning on October 26, to formulate a settlement.

Castro's part in these events is significant. Unquestionably a complete history of the missile crisis must incorporate the Cuban perspective. Yet it is clear that Castro's role was far less important than that of Kennedy or Khrushchev. The idea of putting missiles in Cuba was Khrushchev's. The diplomatic interplay that brought the crisis to an end was essentially Soviet-American. Castro's impact on events was important on only two, perhaps three occasions: first, in the spring of 1962 when he agreed to allow nuclear weapons in Cuba (without his consent there would have been no missiles in Cuba and thus no missile crisis); and, second, at the height of the crisis, when his letter to Khrushchev, suggesting a retaliatory nuclear strike on the United States, may well have enlarged the Soviet leader's desire to end the crisis. Castro's decision to fire on American reconnaissance planes also seems to have encouraged the Soviet military in Cuba to shoot down the U-2 on October 27; and that incident again may have left Khrushchev with the sense that events were getting out of hand and demanded a quick solution.

Despite the caution that Kennedy and Khrushchev showed during the missile crisis, its outcome might still have been disastrous. Luck, as well as their skill, was of vital importance in ensuring a peaceful settlement. It was fortunate that Kennedy had not persuaded the Turks earlier to allow the Jupiters to be withdrawn. This provided an escape hatch during the crisis itself, a concession that Khrushchev could demand and Kennedy could concede. It was fortunate that American intelligence detected the missiles by mid-October. Before then, the Kennedy administration had been accelerating its preparations for military action against Cuba, though JFK had almost certainly not decided to carry out an assault. If the CIA had not discovered the missiles, and Kennedy had decided to invade Cuba unaware that Khrushchev had given General Pliyev permission to attack American forces with Luna missiles, the result could have been catastrophic.

The chief lesson to be learned from the Cuban missile crisis, therefore, does not lie in the area of crisis management—the techniques to be employed in defusing future crises, based on policymakers' experiences in October 1962. Instead these events demonstrate above all else the need to avoid such crises in the first place. Great-power leaders must always consider the long-term consequences of their policies, focusing in particular on how their actions influence those of other statesmen. Had Kennedy and Khrushchev done that in 1961 and 1962, there would be no history of the Cuban missile crisis to write.

A Note on Sources

THE LITERATURE on the Cuban missile crisis is extensive. The two most important early works were Elie Abel, *The Missile Crisis* (Philadelphia, 1966), and Graham T. Allison, *Essence of Decision: Explaining the Cuban Missile Crisis* (New York, 1971). As with many of the first accounts, Abel's focused sharply on the events of October 1962, giving precrisis issues only brief coverage. Allison's study, which develops three models for understanding the missile crisis, is a classic, and still a staple for political scientists. Another early work worth consulting is Henry M. Pachter, *Collision Course: The Cuban Missile Crisis and Coexistence* (New York, 1963).

The key works of the late 1970s were Herbert S. Dinerstein, *The Making of a Missile Crisis, October 1962* (Baltimore, 1976), and David Detzer, *The Brink: Cuban Missile Crisis, 1962* (New York, 1979). Detzer's work was able to utilize then new evidence on Operation Mongoose and the attempts to assassinate Castro. Alexander L. George, "The Cuban Missile Crisis, 1962," in George, David K. Hall, and William E. Simons, *The Limits of Coercive Diplomacy: Laos, Cuba, Vietnam* (Boston, 1971), is a particularly stimulating effort.

A number of significant studies have been produced during the 1980s and 1990s. Raymond L. Garthoff, *Reflections on the Cuban Missile Crisis* (rev. ed., Washington, D.C., 1989), was pathbreaking in the detail it provided on Soviet policymaking. Thomas G. Paterson, "Fixation with Cuba: The Bay of Pigs, Missile Crisis, and Covert War Against Fidel Castro," in Paterson, ed., *Kennedy's Quest for Victory: American Foreign Policy, 1961–1963* (New York, 1989), and Robert Smith Thompson, *The Missiles of October: The Declassified Story of John F. Kennedy and the Cuban Missile Crisis* (New York, 1992), are both critical of JFK's performance. Dino A. Brugioni, *Eyeball to Eyeball: The Inside Story of the Cuban Missile Crisis* (New York, 1991), is more impressive for its detail than its analytical verve. It does provide interesting insights into the role played by American officials working at the National Photographic Interpretation Center. Mark J. White, *The Cuban Missile Crisis* (New York and Basingstoke, 1996), attempts to provide a balanced view. While sharply critical of the policies of Kennedy and Khrushchev before October 1962, it commends them for the skill and caution they showed in defusing the crisis. This study also presents new information on Senator Keating.

For precrisis American policy toward Cuba, three sources are particularly useful. Peter Wyden, *Bay of Pigs: The Untold Story* (New York, 1979), and Trumbull Higgins, *The Perfect Failure: Kennedy, Eisenhower, and the CIA at the Bay of Pigs* (New York, 1989), are solid accounts of the Bay of Pigs. James G. Hershberg, "Before the 'Missiles of October': Did Kennedy Plan a Military Strike Against Cuba?" *Diplomatic History* 14 (Spring 1990), is the best analysis of Kennedy's covert policies—Mongoose, military contingency planning, and the attempts to assassinate Castro.

Hershberg's is only one of a mass of articles to have been written on the missile crisis. Thomas G. Paterson and William J. Brophy, "October Missiles and November Elections: The Cuban Missile Crisis and American Politics, 1962," *Journal of American History* 73 (June 1986), is the definitive study of the relationship between the Cuban crisis and the 1962 congressional elections. The authors cogently argue that Kennedy's Cuban policies were unaffected by those upcoming elections. Philip Nash, "Nuisance of Decision: Jupiter Missiles and the Cuban Missile Crisis," *Journal of Strategic Studies* 14 (1991), is an excellent analysis of the Jupiter issue. Richard Ned Lebow, "Domestic Politics and the Cuban Missile Crisis: The Traditional and Revisionist Interpretations Reevaluated," *Diplomatic History* 14 (Fall 1990), examines the historiography of the missile crisis.

For an attempt to rehabilitate Adlai Stevenson, so often criticized for his performance during the crisis, see Mark J. White, "Hamlet in New York: Adlai Stevenson During the First Week of the Cuban Missile Crisis," *Illinois Historical Journal* 86 (Summer 1993). White, "Belligerent Beginnings: John F. Kennedy on the Opening Day of the Cuban Missile Crisis," *Journal of Strategic Studies* 15 (March 1992), shows that JFK strongly favored an air strike at the start of the crisis and thus needed to be persuaded by his advisers to switch his support to the blockade option. White, "Dean Rusk's Revelation: New British Evidence on the Cordier Ploy," *Society for Historians of American Foreign Relations Newsletter* 25 (September 1994), presents important information on the Cordier ploy from the Public Record Office.

There are two exceedingly useful anthologies: Robert A. Divine, ed., *The Cuban Missile Crisis* (Chicago, 1971), and James A. Nathan, ed., *The Cuban Missile Crisis Revisited* (New York, 1992). The Nathan volume includes Barton J. Bernstein's excellent "Reconsidering the Missile Crisis: Dealing with the Problems of the American Jupiters in Turkey," and Philip Brenner, "Thirteen Months: Cuba's Perspective on the Missile Crisis," an essay that adds to our understanding of Havana's role in the events of 1962.

For a proper understanding of John Kennedy's role in the Cuban missile crisis, his background and prepresidential career must be considered. The two best works here are Nigel Hamilton, *JFK: Reckless Youth* (New York, 1992), and Herbert S. Parmet, *Jack: The Struggles of John F. Kennedy* (New York, 1980). The general evaluations of JFK's life and presidency provide radically different interpretations. Arthur M. Schlesinger, Jr., *A Thousand Days: John F. Kennedy in the White House* (Boston, 1965), and Theodore C. Sorensen, *Kennedy* (New York, 1965) are beautifully written tributes—the classic works of the "Camelot" school. For studies at the opposite end of the spectrum, see the fiercely critical Garry Wills, *The Kennedy Imprisonment: A Meditation on Power* (Boston and Toronto, 1982), and Thomas C. Reeves, *A Question of Character: A Life of John F. Kennedy* (New

York, 1991). James N. Giglio, *The Presidency of John F. Kennedy* (Lawrence, Kans., 1991), and Herbert S. Parmet, *JFK: The Presidency of John F. Kennedy* (New York, 1983), are pleasingly balanced. For a recent account, see the richly detailed Richard Reeves, *President Kennedy: Profile of Power* (New York, 1993).

The two best general accounts of Kennedy's foreign policy are Michael R. Beschloss, *The Crisis Years: Kennedy and Khrushchev, 1960–1963* (New York, 1991), and Thomas G. Paterson, ed., *Kennedy's Quest for Victory* (New York, 1989). Of the two, Paterson's volume is more comprehensive in scope and more hostile in interpretation.

Many officials who participated in the Cuban missile crisis have written memoirs. The papers of others have been published. Most famous and useful is Robert F. Kennedy, *Thirteen Days: A Memoir of the Cuban Missile Crisis* (New York, 1969). Readers should be aware of Theodore Sorensen's acknowledgment in 1989 that he had helped write the book by editing Robert Kennedy's diary of the missile crisis—and in so doing had removed parts of it that indicated the attorney general had made an explicit commitment in his October 27 meeting with Dobrynin on the removal of the Jupiter missiles from Turkey.

Many other memoirs and published papers are of great value. These include George W. Ball, *The Past Has Another Pattern: Memoirs* (New York, 1982); McGeorge Bundy, *Danger and Survival: Choices About the Bomb in the First Fifty Years* (New York, 1988); Walter Johnson, ed., *The Papers of Adlai E. Stevenson,* vol. 8 (Boston, 1979); Paul H. Nitze, with Ann M. Smith and Steven L. Rearden, *From Hiroshima to Glasnost: At the Center of Decision* (New York, 1989); Kenneth P. O'Donnell and David F. Powers, with Joe McCarthy, *"Johnny, We Hardly Knew Ye": Memories of John Fitzgerald Kennedy* (Boston, 1972); Dean Rusk, as told to Richard Rusk, *As I Saw It* (New York, 1990); Pierre Salinger, *With Kennedy* (Garden City, N.Y., 1966); Schlesinger, *A Thousand Days;* and Sorensen, *Kennedy.*

The most important Soviet reminiscences are to be found in

Nikita S. Khrushchev's three volumes of memoirs: *Khrushchev Remembers* (Boston, 1970); *Khrushchev Remembers: The Last Testament* (Boston, 1974); and *Khrushchev Remembers: The Glasnost Tapes* (Boston, 1990). Other accounts by former Soviet officials are to be found in Fedor Burlatsky, *Khrushchev and the First Russian Spring* (London, 1991), and parts of Anatoli I. Gribkov and William Y. Smith, *Operation ANADYR: U.S. and Soviet Generals Recount the Cuban Missile Crisis* (Chicago, 1994). See also Anatoly Dobrynin, "The Caribbean Crisis: An Eyewitness Account," *International Affairs* 8 (August 1992), and Oleg Troyanovsky, "The Caribbean Crisis: A View from the Kremlin," *International Affairs* 4-5 (April–May 1992).

The Cuban missile crisis has generated a huge amount of published documentation, more than virtually any other topic in the field of U.S. foreign relations. This means that many of the key documents may be examined by students and teachers without having to journey to faraway archives. Most useful is Laurence Chang and Peter Kornbluh, eds., *The Cuban Missile Crisis, 1962: A Documents Reader* (New York, 1992), a collection which includes materials on Operation Mongoose and other precrisis issues as well as on the crisis itself. U.S. Central Intelligence Agency, *The Secret Cuban Missile Crisis Documents* (Washington, D.C., 1994), has important materials on the role played by the CIA, especially its director, John McCone. Tapes and transcripts of various ExComm meetings are available from the John F. Kennedy Library.

At a series of conferences in the past decade, former officials and scholars have discussed the missile crisis. This has produced not only interesting reflections but startling revelations, particularly on the issues of the Luna missiles in Cuba and the Cordier ploy. Transcripts of these conferences and some useful commentaries are provided for the 1987 conferences held in the United States in James G. Blight and David A. Welch, *On the Brink: Americans and Soviets Reexamine the Cuban Missile Crisis* (New York, 1990); for the 1989 Moscow conference in Bruce J. Allyn,

Blight, and Welch, eds., *Back to the Brink: Proceedings of the Moscow Conference on the Cuban Missile Crisis, January 27–28, 1989* (Lanham, Md., 1992); and for the 1992 Havana conference, which Castro himself attended, in Blight, Allyn, and Welch, *Cuba on the Brink: Castro, the Missile Crisis, and the Soviet Collapse* (New York, 1993). This latter work is also important for the way it argues that a comprehensive history of the missile crisis must include proper coverage of the Cuban role.

For the most recent documents released in Russia, see the *Cold War International History Project Bulletin*, a publication of the Woodrow Wilson Center. Especially useful is issue 5 (Spring 1995), which includes the correspondence between Soviet officials in Moscow and those in Washington, Havana, and New York, both before and during the missile crisis. Dobrynin's reports on his October 23 and 27 meetings with Robert Kennedy are particularly helpful. For new information from Russian archives on Scali's contacts with Feklisov, see, in the same issue, Alexander Fursenko and Timothy Naftali, "Using KGB Documents: The Scali-Feklisov Channel in the Cuban Missile Crisis." Fresh materials on the Luna issue are exploited in issue 3 (Fall 1993) in Mark Kramer, "Tactical Nuclear Weapons, Soviet Command Authority, and the Cuban Missile Crisis," and in Blight, Allyn, and Welch, "Kramer vs. Kramer."

For a record of everything that Kennedy said in public during his presidency, including his statements on Cuba, see U.S. National Archives and Records Service, *Public Papers of the Presidents of the United States: John F. Kennedy, 1961–1963* (Washington, D.C., 1962–1964). Rusk's public comments on Cuba may be found in U.S. Department of State, *Press Conferences of the Secretaries of State*, series III, reel no. 14, January 1958–December 1965. The findings of the 1975 Senate investigation into the CIA's attempts to eliminate Castro (and other leaders) are presented in U.S. Senate Select Committee to Study Governmental Operations with Respect to Intelligence Activities, *Alleged Assassination*

Plots Involving Foreign Leaders, interim report, S. Rept. 94-465, 94th Congress, 1st session.

I have also made use of archival materials. The two key depositories are the John F. Kennedy Library in Boston and the National Security Archive in Washington, D.C. For the Kennedy Library, the important collections are the National Security Files, President's Office Files, Oral History Collection, and the Papers of Theodore Sorensen and Arthur M. Schlesinger, Jr. The National Security Archive has produced a microfiche collection containing thousands of pages of documents. Students and scholars should note, however, that many additional items declassified since the publication of that collection, including important documents on Operation Mongoose, are available at the National Security Archive at George Washington University.

A number of other manuscript collections are of supplementary value. The Papers of Adlai Stevenson at Princeton University and of Dean Acheson at the Harry S. Truman Library in Independence, Missouri, shed light on the roles played by those two individuals. The Vice-Presidential Security Files at the Lyndon Baines Johnson Library in Austin, Texas, contain notes taken by Johnson during the ExComm meetings. The Allen Dulles Papers at Princeton are important for an understanding of the issue of whether JFK was briefed during the 1960 campaign about the planning for what later became the Bay of Pigs operation. For Kennedy's consultations with Eisenhower, see the Post-Presidential Papers at the Dwight D. Eisenhower Library in Abilene, Kansas. The Papers of Kenneth Keating, the key figure in the Republican assault on JFK in the fall of 1962, are located at the University of Rochester, Rochester, New York. I have also used the key British archive for government documents, the Public Record Office in Kew, London. The materials there reveal much about U.S. policy toward Cuba before and during the missile crisis, as well as the British perspective on events.

Index

A NOTE ON THE AUTHOR

Mark J. White is assistant professor of history at Eastern Illinois University. Born in Holbrook, England, he studied at the University of Nottingham, the University of Wisconsin, Milwaukee, and Rutgers University, where he received a Ph.D. He has written widely on American foreign policy and is also the author of *The Cuban Missile Crisis*.